100 PHOTOS
THAT CHANGED CANADA

100
PHOTOS
THAT CHANGED
CANADA

EDITED BY MARK REID, *THE BEAVER* MAGAZINE
FOREWORD BY CHARLOTTE GRAY
PREFACE BY DEBORAH MORRISON

HarperCollins*PublishersLtd*
A PHYLLIS BRUCE BOOK

100 Photos That Changed Canada
Copyright © 2009. All rights reserved.

Published by HarperCollins Publishers Ltd

First edition

HarperCollins books may be purchased for educational, business, or sales promotional use through our Special Markets Department.

HarperCollins Publishers Ltd
2 Bloor Street East, 20th Floor
Toronto, Ontario, Canada
M4W 1A8

www.harpercollins.ca

Library and Archives Canada Cataloguing in Publication
100 photos that changed Canada/Canada's National
History Society; edited by Mark Reid; foreword by Charlotte
Gray and Deborah Morrison.

ISBN 978-1-55468-497-7

1. Canada–History–Pictorial works. I. Reid, Mark
II. Canada's National History Society III. Title.
IV. Title: One hundred photos that changed Canada.

FC59.O57 2009   971.0022'2   C2009-903101-9

P+ 9 8 7 6 5 4 3 2

Printed and bound in China

Original montage concept:
Michel Groleau

Copy-editing:
Phil Koch
Nelle Oosterom
Beverley Tallon

Contents

LIST OF PHOTOS

LIST OF PHOTOGRAPHERS

This book is dedicated to the hard-working photographers who stopped the world to show us what matters. Some of these people are known and celebrated; others are anonymous, lost in the mists of time. Among them are

Gérard Aimé

Scott Applewhite

Doug Ball

Stan Behal

Jim Brandenburg

Murray Brewster

B. Brooks

Oliver B. Buell

Ron Bull

Duncan Cameron

William Ivor Castle

T.A. Chandler

Fred Chartrand

Paul Chiasson

Ted Church

Antoine Claudet

Albert Crookshank

Fred Davis

Jack DeLorme

Claude P. Detloff

Kevoek Djansezian

Thomas Coffin Doane

Robert Flaherty

L.B. Foote

Ray Giguere

Wayne Glowacki

Ted Grant

Fred Greenslade

Frank Gunn

James Inglis

William James

Yousuf Karsh

Robert Keziere

Shaney Komulainen

Frank Lennon

Alexander Ross

Wallace R. MacAskill

Larry MacDougal

Rod MacIvor

Alexander Mackenzie Stirton

Peter Martin

Allen McInnis

Charles Mitchell

Gilbert Alexander Milne

J.F. Moran

Robert Nadon

Phil Nolan

William Notman

Bob Olsen

Barry Philp

Ryan Remiorz

George P. Roberts

Dimo Safari

Jarome Silberstein

Roger St-Jean

Tak Toyota

Mark van Manen

Barbara Woodley

John Thomas Woodruff

A full list of photo credits can be found on p. 225.

Charlotte Gray

Can a photo change a country? Looking through the powerful images in this collection, the answer is "yes." Scenes of joy and shame, triumph and tragedy—each of these one hundred photos has changed the way we think about Canada.

Photographs freeze a moment in time as life speeds on and that moment lodges in our collective memory. An image may not have the dramatic, real-time impact of a battle, an economic crisis, or a political victory. But these photos have shaped our perceptions of what we value, or whom we admire, or why this vast federation sprawled atop a superpower has survived and thrived.

Some of these photographs are seared on our eyeballs—think of the nose-to-nose standoff between a Canadian soldier and a Mohawk warrior at Oka, Quebec, in 1990. There are images of triumph and achievement, and of horror. Many of the photographs will provoke viscerally dissimilar reactions from different viewers. The driving of the "Last Spike" for a transcontinental railway in 1885, for example, symbolizes a nation-building achievement for some Canadians—and an ugly reminder of sweated labour and a land grab to others. There is always more than one side to every story, every image—and in a country as complex as Canada, that means that our history is full of troublesome conflicts and hard-won compromises.

Photography predates our country's emergence as an independent dominion, yet its development has neatly paralleled that of Canada. Pioneer photographers were eager to record the moment, but the technical demands of primitive cameras stretched the moment to minutes. So the earliest images here are staged portraits, lending them a gravitas that reinforces the importance of the sitters and the occasion.

These photos record events as the governmental and social elites of the day intended them to be seen—as myth-making moments in a national drama. In the late nineteenth century, a handful of politicians and lawyers stitched this country together while, offstage, thousands of farmers, fishers, city-dwellers and members of First Nations strove to survive. Photography, at this stage, was out of their reach.

Fast-forward to an era with more voices included in the national dialogue, and more spontaneity in the art of photography. As decades progressed, we increasingly looked to photography to capture unpleasant—as well as historic—truths. Photographers created images that helped define individual and national character. The inclusive accessibility of photography today matches the inclusive accessibility of Canada's national cultures. Inevitably, this has led to the "gotcha!" sensationalism that permeates today's tabloids. But it has also meant that the camera's lens has captured and celebrated the extraordinary heterogeneity of Canada's peoples and traditions.

A country is defined in its citizens' psyches by its shared symbols, ethics, and memories. *100 Photos That Changed Canada* captures unforgettable moments in our country's journey into the future. These images remind us who we are.

PREFACE

Deborah Morrison

This book—*100 Photos That Changed Canada*—began as a brilliantly whimsical idea on the part of our editor, Mark Reid, for a summer 2008 issue of our flagship magazine, *The Beaver*. He invited top Canadian photographers and photo editors to help identify the ten most important photographs in Canadian history. The magazine article became a public exhibit, and the exhibit happily led to this book project.

This book is first and foremost a tribute to Canada's photographers, whose work provides us with a texture and a context to our past that we often take for granted. However, Mark's timely project to explore Canada's most iconic photographs has led many of us into deeper reflections on the importance of these images to historical research, of where these images are kept, and of who is able to see them.

The project has been a labour of love for Mark and the incredibly hard-working staff at Canada's National History Society. We're proud of their efforts, along with those of the journalists, writers, and historians who've so generously contributed to the project.

Indeed, bringing Canada's stories vividly to life has been the mission of the History Society and *The Beaver* since the Hudson's Bay Company first launched the magazine as a company newsletter in October 1920. Today, it has evolved to become *Canada's History Magazine*.

Publishing *The Beaver* is just one aspect of the History Society's mission: to promote popular interest in Canadian history. The History Society also rewards and recognizes excellence in history within the educational community—through our Governor General's Awards—and in popular media—through the Pierre Berton Award. We have developed programs and resources for use both inside and outside of the classroom, in print and online.

The Beaver has long used photographs to help make our stories come to life. We've encouraged readers to share their personal histories through images in the magazine's "Album" section; taught young children how to "read a picture" through *Kayak: Canada's History Magazine for Kids'* regular "Bubbleology" feature; and created a rich repository of digital images bringing the HBC museum and archive collections to researchers and classrooms around the world.

These photos often come from professional sources, such as archives. However, equally valuable are the personal photographs of ordinary Canadians—those visual treasures that have been carefully stored in a shoebox before being rediscovered years or decades later. It is these photos that give us all a true sense of our everyday past.

During our eighty-nine years in operation, we've experienced a revolution in the way photographs are captured, stored, reproduced, and shared. The availability of images has never been greater—but photographic records have never been in a more precarious state. Few of us still dutifully keep detailed notes on the backs of our personal photographs. Decades of negatives (remember those?) have been lost. And today, millions of digital photos are being tucked away in anonymous computer folders. What photographs will we have to tell today's stories tomorrow?

We hope this book will inspire you to think about your own photos and memories, and encourage you to share them with those around you. But above all, we hope you will enjoy this incredible collection of memories, and that you'll see it as we've come to—as a veritable family album for a nation. Welcome to the family!

MARIANNE HELM

INTRODUCTION

Mark Reid

Somewhere between light entering a lens and the release of the shutter, amid the alchemy of f-stops and aperture adjustments, great photographs are born. The greatest photos are those that affect us in some way and offer insights into the subjects that are hidden from the naked eye.

It was the master Canadian photographer Yousuf Karsh who once said, "Within every man and woman a secret is hidden, and as a photographer it is my task to reveal it if I can." The question is: Can photographs reveal the secret to understanding a country so vast and diverse as Canada?

100 Photos That Changed Canada is not so much a history book as it is a search for the shared moments—the terrible and the sublime— in which we frame the notion of who we are as a people and a nation.

From the outset, we knew that we wanted this book to be unlike any other photo history of Canada. We wanted our contributors to view the images in this collection through a different lens—a lens both passionate and analytical—and answer the question that will be asked of every single photograph in this book: Who cares?

Who cares that early in the twentieth century women across Canada fought for, and won, the right to vote? Who cares that a one-legged young man had the audacity to think he could end cancer by running across Canada? And why does it matter that, in the dying seconds of a hockey game in Moscow, a Canadian player banged in his own rebound—vaulting his team from ignominy to immortality?

In 2008, *The Beaver* featured a story called "10 Photos That Changed Canada." On the cover was a photo of Terry Fox in silhouette, running along a rain-slicked road in Ontario in July 1980. Accompanying Terry's photo were these words: "Some filled us with pride, others brought us to tears. These are the images that shaped our nation."

Sifting through hundreds of photographs in search of the best for this collection, we came to see that Canada has many iconic images. All of the photos in this book have, in some way, shaped our perceptions of Canada and of ourselves. They're a tangible reminder of the collective triumphs, failures, and sacrifices experienced by Canadians throughout the years.

If there is a universal truth to be found in this compilation, it's this: History lives only as long as there are those willing to remember it. Great photographs are not only a vivid and visual reminder of our past, they are a means to preserve it.

This collection of *100 Photos That Changed Canada* is by no means a definitive list. It's a snapshot of who we were, who we are, and who we might become.

100 PHOTOS
THAT CHANGED CANADA

PART ONE

THE ROAD
TO NATIONHOOD

1847-1921

We were a young Dominion when our eyes first turned collectively to the West, spurred on by the brash notion of a nation stretching from sea to sea. And as rails of steel started stretching toward the horizon, it seemed anything was possible.

Canadians soon grew more connected—for better and for worse. Cultures and ambitions clashed on the Plains. Indigenous peoples suffered, and entire ways of life disappeared. Newcomers rushed to stake a claim to this fledgling nation. Some were lured by gold, others by the flickering hope of making a fresh start in the New World.

A final hammer blow, struck in 1885 in Craigellachie, B.C., did more than fix a railway tie to earth—it tied together East and West.

As we journeyed along the road to nationhood, a new technology had arisen, one that could fix a moment in time and hold it fast for future generations. The first "permanent" photograph was taken in France in the 1820s. The invention of the daguerreotype followed in 1839.

Soon, Canadians were taking up the strange new device and setting out across the country to capture history in action. In Montreal, William Notman—one of the early masters—was experimenting with "composite images" by photographing dozens of individual subjects and then combining them into larger scenes. Photographers everywhere were hauling their cumbersome cameras and tripods to record events both great and small.

Until then, Canadians had relied on painters to be their window on momentous events. The trouble was, the scenes they painted were often infused with brushstrokes of bias and exaggeration. The camera showed Canadians the world as it was, and what drama there was to see: the female daredevil who defeated Niagara Falls; a record-breaking foot race; even the moment when Canada joined the age of flight. Photographers would be there when Canadian soldiers went to war in Europe, and also there to witness strife on the home front as workers fought—and in some cases, died—for their rights. Cameras would help create new icons and hit home the horror of disasters.

The impact of this new visual medium was immediate and far-reaching. The blinkers were off. The world, viewed through the camera's lens, could at times be terrible, but it could also be beautiful.

As the Great War ended, we were relieved, yet unsure of what the future would hold. One thing was certain: Thanks to photography, the way we viewed ourselves, and our nation, had forever changed.

—Mark Reid

1

Aboriginal chief Maun-gua-daus, 1847.

Between Two Worlds

The man who struggled to know himself

JIM BURANT

This is a portrait of a man caught between two worlds. While he appears poised and full of confidence, he was actually in the midst of an identity crisis of profound dimensions. And even though he published accounts of his life, we know little about him.

Maun-gua-daus—his Ojibway name, which he translated as "great hero" or "courageous"—was born in Forty Mile Creek, Upper Canada, possibly in 1807 or in 1811. He was Christianized and baptized George Henry. While raised in traditional aboriginal ways, he also attended a Methodist mission school in York (now Toronto). He would later accompany missionary parties as an interpreter, help write an Ojibway hymn book, and preach at missions.

In 1840, George Henry made a significant life change. He left the ministry, apparently disillusioned with Methodist politics. By 1843, he had lost his job as an interpreter and needed to find a way to support his family. After hearing reports of troupes of "wild Indians" touring Europe, George Henry assembled his own group of native performers, which toured America in 1844 before sailing for Europe. Reclaiming the name Maun-gua-daus, he and his troupe arrived in England in March 1845 and performed for enthusiastic audiences in London, Paris, and Brussels. The European tour would be struck by tragedy, however. Smallpox claimed three of the performers, while in 1846, Maun-gua-daus lost three of his children, likely to tuberculosis. Then, in December 1847, his wife died of unknown causes. By 1848, the troupe had returned to America, with only five of the original twelve members still alive.

It is in this context that one can look at this amazing portrait, likely taken between spring 1846 and December 1847, when Maun-gua-daus would have been about thirty-five to forty years of age. He looks preoccupied and serious, and is wearing a costume that combines a European-style cloth coat with native beadwork and trimming, as well as one of the medals presented to him by King Louis-Philippe of France. There is a hint of play-acting in the pose, almost as if he was uncertain about who he was or where he would be going.

This is a unique and invaluable image, not solely because it is one of the earliest surviving daguerreotypes of any Canadian extant, but also because of Maun-gau-daus's story as he struggled with his identity and sense of self.

Maun-gua-daus assimilated and became George Henry, Methodist preacher—then turned back into Maun-gua-daus, and met royalty, nobility, and a wide range of famous people. But in the process he exposed his family to disease and death. His troupe ceased touring in the early 1850s, and Maun-gua-daus himself eventually became a herbalist and native doctor with the Mississaugas of the New Credit First Nation. There is no record of when he died.

His personal history reflects the struggle of many aboriginal persons in the nineteenth century to assimilate into a society that not all loved. This image represents a pivotal moment in the history of Canada's First Nations and is a microcosmic example of contemporary attitudes in Western society towards the fate of North America's aboriginal peoples.

Up from the Ashes

Early disaster image offered glimpse of things to come

BRIAN YOUNG

One of the first examples of photojournalism in Canada, this photo combines one of the staples of successful photojournalism—the disaster—with human interest—the posing of presumed victims, in this case a gentleman, woman, and child.

The violence, colour, and destructive quality of fire have fascinated all humans, in all times. New technologies, such as the telegraph and the daguerreotype photograph, ensured that news of the huge Montreal fire of July 9, 1852, could be shared around the British Empire. Leaving some 10,000 homeless, it burned much of the city's east end, including 1,100 homes and the new Roman Catholic cathedral.

For its part, the Molson's Brewery—established in 1786 and the oldest continuously operating brewery in North America—was a Montreal landmark, as synonymous with the city as John Labatt's Brewery was with London, Ontario. While we do not know who the man in the photo is, we can speculate that he is John Henry Robinson Molson, grandson of founder John Molson and proprietor of the brewery after 1848. Besides the brewery, the fire burned several Molson homes and the Anglican church the family had sponsored.

The gentleman's pose, standing among the ruins in top hat and suit, suggests authority and perhaps a vision of phoenix rising from the ashes. Typical of the period and the secondary place accorded to women, the Molsons, as potential purchasers of this memorabilia, may have been pleased with this image of woman and child, seated, patient, and waiting on male authority.

The photo was published in the *Illustrated London News*. Established in 1842, this magazine was an immediate success, a Victorian tabloid-like precursor of *Life*, *Look*, or *Paris Match*. Focusing on British royalty, public spectacles—such as the Duke of Wellington's funeral—and disasters, it dispatched photographers with war correspondents and traditional artists to the Crimean war zone in 1854. In one of its first editions, it published a photo of the great Hamburg fire of May 4, 1842, which destroyed 1,000 dwellings. Colour foldouts were reproduced from the magazine, framed, and sold to decorate Victorian living rooms.

Thomas Coffin Doane (1814–96), the man who shot this image, was an early daguerreotype photographer with studios in Montreal and St. John's, Newfoundland. Despite his well-known portraits of the Patriote Louis-Joseph Papineau and of Governor General Lord Elgin, he was less successful in establishing a commercial photographic business than his contemporaries, William Notman in Montreal and Jules-Isaïe Livernois in Quebec City. This photo, however, gives Doane rank in the first generation of photojournalists.

It also gave Victorian readers a glimpse of an exciting and new visual future: one in which—thanks to photography—breaking news events could now be reproduced and disseminated around the world.

2

Aftermath of the Molson's Brewery fire in Montreal, 1852.

The Fathers of Confederation in Charlottetown, September 1864.

Canada's Father Figures

Delegates built Confederation to last

MICHAEL BLISS

If these are the Fathers of Confederation, where are the Mothers?

The complete absence of women as delegates to the 1864 Charlottetown Conference that gave birth to the Dominion of Canada on July 1, 1867, is one of the most striking impressions this classic photo makes on today's Canadians. It was an all-male political world in the nineteenth century; women did not even have the right to vote.

Then again, not even male voters were asked to ratify the handiwork of the politicians who began devising a new federation during a week of meetings and convivial socializing in the capital of Prince Edward Island that September. They met again a month later in Quebec, put the scheme to their legislatures for approval, had a third conference in London, England, in 1866, and finally had Confederation passed into law by the British Parliament as the British North America Act.

By that time, several of the provinces had held deeply divisive internal debates about the scheme. Prince Edward Island, where it had been born, decided it had no interest in joining the mainland, and stayed out of Confederation until 1873. Nova Scotians' first reaction to becoming Canadians was to petition Britain to be allowed to secede. Newfoundlanders were not part of official Canadian pictures until 1949.

It's a sign of our historical tolerance, or our acceptance of the inevitable, that we tend to count as Fathers of Confederation every delegate to the three confederation conferences, even the politicians who opposed and fought against the scheme, and even the two Newfoundland politicians who were merely observers at the Quebec Conference.

It's asking too much of even Canadian schoolchildren that they should have to memorize the names of the Fathers of Confederation, or be able to identify the twenty-five politicians in this picture. The group includes all the best-known Fathers: Charles Tupper from Nova Scotia, Charles Tilley from New Brunswick, George-Étienne Cartier, George Brown, Alexander Tilloch Galt, and, above all, John A. Macdonald from the then-Province of Canada (later Ontario and Quebec). Macdonald, who became the principal architect of Confederation and Canada's first prime minister, is seated in the centre of the picture; Cartier, his Quebec lieutenant, stands facing him at his right hand.

What an imposing building—Prince Edward Island's Government House—hosts the delegates on this occasion. Colonials built well in the nineteenth century, solid structures meant to last. If Canada and its public buildings have common denominators, it is their great strength and staying power. Even the skeptics understood the need for strong foundations, classic pillars, and room to grow.

Mourning a Martyr

Profound grief followed first political assassination

JIM BURANT

In the pre-dawn hours of an April evening in 1868, a man makes his way back to his lodgings after a long night of work. Thomas D'Arcy McGee, member of Canada's Parliament, erstwhile Irish revolutionary, Liberal reformer, and now part of the ruling Conservative party, reaches the door of his lodgings and prepares to turn the key in the lock. But an unknown assailant steps out of the shadows and shoots him dead. McGee is the first Canadian politician ever assassinated, and a nation is thrown into turmoil.

McGee was just shy of his forty-third birthday when he was murdered by a suspected Irish Fenian. But he had already led a tumultuous and adventurous life. In his youth he left Ireland, moved to Boston and joined an Irish nationalist newspaper. In this position he advocated Irish independence from Britain, and the annexation of Canada by the United States.

He would return to Ireland and take part in the unsuccessful Irish rebellion of 1848. Forced to flee, by 1857 he was living in Montreal. By this time, he had abandoned his support for Irish independence, and was soon elected to the Legislative Assembly of Canada. He became a passionate advocate of Confederation, and made many enemies in the Irish independence movement, including the Fenians. The Fenians were Irish-American Civil War veterans who sought to capture Canada in order to force the British government to give Ireland its independence.

It was in this context that McGee's assassination took place. Although McGee was not universally beloved in life, his death caused an outpouring of grief across the nation. He was viewed as one of the Fathers of Confederation and had become a martyr in the cause of Canadian unity. He was given a state funeral in Montreal on April 13, 1868, with thousands lining the streets to pay their respects.

This photograph, taken by the Montreal photographer James Inglis, is notable for a number of reasons. Probably taken from the balcony of a building as the procession passed, it was a technical triumph, as he was able, due to a rapid emulsion, to capture a large crowd in motion instantaneously. The image was widely sold and was also published in the *Illustrated London News* on May 9, 1868, making it available to a worldwide audience numbering in the millions. James Inglis opened a studio in Montreal in 1866 and went on to become a technical innovator of great importance. He died in 1904 from the effects of injuries caused by using flash powder to take a photograph.

Inglis's photograph of McGee's funeral is a masterpiece, with the catafalque pulled by a large team of horses occupying the left centre of the image. He must have waited for the precise moment to capture the image, since the cortège would have gone from view in another few seconds. This was Inglis's only chance to capture a key moment in Canada's history, and he got it right.

4

The funeral procession of Thomas D'Arcy McGee,
Montreal, April 13, 1868.

William Notman's "Skating Carnival,"
a painted composite shot in 1870.

Marvellous Montage

Master photographer made magic with his lens

DENYS DELÂGE

On March 1, 1870, Montreal's anglophone elite attended a Mardi Gras skating carnival held in honour of Prince Arthur, Queen Victoria's youngest son. The prince is shown in the foreground of this image in the lower left corner, face unobstructed. Organizers had decorated the Victoria Skating Rink in colonial colours, and on the balcony and large platform surrounding the ice surface crowds of spectators watched skaters dressed in magnificent costumes.

During Mardi Gras, the world as we know it is turned upside down, and this photo illustrates that well—a gigantic teacup is centre stage, and everywhere historical figures and people are mingling. Among them are highlanders and peasants, a veiled lady of the evening with a moon headdress (centre), Diana "goddess of the hunt," an aboriginal person with bow and arrow, and a scandalous scene!—a lady smoking a cigar in public (lower right corner).

What's most amazing about this image, however, is that it isn't real. It's a montage of dozens of separate photographs, masterfully arranged to recreate the magic of the actual skating party.

This groundbreaking composite image was created by William Notman, who is today considered one of the greatest photographers of his era. Born in Scotland in 1826, Notman settled in Montreal in 1856 and quickly earned a reputation as a master photographer. He photographed wealthy families, the Fathers of Confederation, as well as many of the important events that showcased Canadian society in the mid to late 1800s. One of Notman's most famous photographs was of the construction of the then-longest bridge in the world—the Victoria Bridge that connects Montreal to the South Shore. Queen Victoria was so enamoured with his work that she declared him "Photographer to the Queen." His innovations with composite images such as this one would influence an entire generation of photographers.

Notman's skating carnival image was his first large-scale composite photograph. To create the image, he invited to his studio more than 150 individuals and small groups, dressed in their costumes and skates. He then photographed them in a variety of positions. Using an enlarger (with the sun as its light source), Notman projected the final image onto a photosensitive canvas, which was later painted by artists.

Notman's photos won many international awards, and he paved the way for photography to be considered a form of artistic expression. However, although his photographs captured many beautiful scenes, his work, like that of most of his contemporaries, remained blind to the misery and epidemics of his era.

A gifted entrepreneur, he established twenty-six studios across North America. After his death, his sons managed the businesses until 1935. Bequeathed to the McCord Museum in Montreal, the Notman Archives consist of 450,000 photographs spanning nearly eight decades. This exceptional collection provides an important visual history of landscapes, portraits, and events that took place in Montreal, Quebec, and Canada.

Steel Will

Railways helped government exert control over country

TIM COOK

The centre does not hold.

This was Sir John A. Macdonald's problem in late 1884, as the messianic, unstable, and enthralling Louis Riel returned to Canada to lead an uprising of Métis in the North West.

Macdonald feared that Riel's Métis would incite aboriginals in the region to join in the fight. Any conflict might hurt immigration and investments, as well as provide the Americans with an excuse to occupy the centre of the young Dominion.

The campaign to put down the Métis was one of logistical challenges rather than a military obstacle. While the Métis were feared for their hunting and sharp-shooting skills, they faced an overwhelming number of militia forces enlisting from Ontario, and to a lesser extent other provinces; the Métis had little hope in this uneven fight.

The challenge, in a country as a large and undeveloped as Canada, was getting the troops quickly to Batoche, in present-day Saskatchewan, where Riel's forces were stationed.

Fortunately for Macdonald, he had the railway. It would have been extremely difficult, whether by foot or on horseback, to move men, supplies, and heavy guns through snow-covered and soggy Shield country and prairie in early spring. However, while nearly completed, there were still four gaps in the Canadian Pacific Railway line, spanning roughly 160 kilometres. The 3,000 or so militia men who went west by rail starting at the end of March suffered severely from the wind, snow, and freezing rain as they marched across the gaps or were ferried by horse teams and sleighs. In other spots along the line, the troops were transported in open railway cars. Arthur Potvin, a medical student with the 9th Voltigeurs, was almost driven to suicide, while another man deliberately had his foot crushed under a train's wheel. The ragged and dispirited force finally arrived in late April and quickly converged on Riel's forces in three columns.

As history tells us, the Canadian militia would eventually defeat the Métis forces, and Riel would be captured on May 15.

Ordered to stand trial in Regina, Riel was taken there by train under an armed escort. That escort is captured in this May 22, 1885, photo by Montreal photographer Oliver Buell. Reclining in their seats, these troops from a Winnipeg field battery enjoyed a comfortable trip to Regina compared with the punishing movement west by Ontario militiamen two months earlier.

The Riel rebellion—or resistance, as some scholars call it—would be the last major armed insurrection on Canadian soil until the Oka Crisis in 1990.

With the CPR linking the country by the end of the year, Macdonald would turn his sight towards building a strong country based on heavy immigration and internal trade, with goods moved along the railway lines. And when war came in the next century, Canada would respond by sending expeditionary forces to battlefields around the world—but it first drew its soldiers from across the country and transported them to the coasts by rail.

Canadian troops escorting Louis Riel catch some sleep, May 22–23, 1885.

6

7

Louis Riel addressing the court during his trial for treason, July 31, 1885.

Reluctant Hero

Riel trial inflamed passions on all sides

DENYS DELÂGE

On July 31, 1885, Louis Riel stood facing six jurors who would soon retire to determine their verdict. In a tiny courtroom in Regina—at the time, the capital of the Northwest Territories—dignitaries and their wives, police and military personnel all packed together to witness the trial of Riel. Charged with high treason under the English law of 1352, he faced a mandatory death sentence.

Riel, in broken English, rejected a plea of insanity that was argued by his lawyers. Calm, composed, and confident, this remarkable speaker highlighted his vulnerability before the court by comparing it to the day of his birth, when his mother was too weak to care for him alone. Would the Northwest Territories—his mother country—care for him as well as had his real mother? He spoke passionately about his return to the Territories in 1884, where he witnessed the physical and spiritual suffering of the aboriginal peoples, the sickness and starvation afflicting the Métis, and the lack of democratic liberties.

He challenged the court to answer *his* questions: Did he not work to unite all people, despite class, cultural identity, and religion? As founder of Manitoba, did Riel not send numerous petitions to the Government of Canada opposing the dispossession of its first inhabitants and demanding the right to a responsible government? Did Ottawa not respond to these requests by using police and military oppression? Riel told the court that, as a prophet of the New World, he was only fulfilling his duty to defend his homeland.

After deliberation, the jury rendered a guilty verdict with a recommendation of mercy, but the judge refused it. On November 16, 1885, Riel was hanged. The entire proceedings of the unjust trial were orchestrated to ensure his execution.

The trials held for the Cree chiefs who fought at the same time as the Métis uprising were just as flawed. The Cree leader Mistahi-Muskwa (Big Bear), along with fourteen of his warriors, was sentenced to three years in prison. The same verdict was handed down to Pitikwahanapi-wiyin (Poundmaker) for confronting police and armed parties in the region of Battleford, Saskatchewan. Finally, on November 27, 1885, Kapapamahchakwew (Wandering Spirit) and five of his associates were hanged for a deadly raid on a Hudson's Bay Company post in Frog Lake, Saskatchewan.

Defeat was at hand and the "West was tamed!" The buffalo had been exterminated, epidemics had devastated the native populations, the railroad now crossed the country, and the colonists had arrived. The Métis soon began to disperse, and aboriginals were rounded up into impoverished reserves. Both groups faced an uncertain future filled with humiliation and abuse of power. The rights of those who were there before the arrival of Canada were squashed under a policy of homogenization. Canada missed the opportunity to embrace multinationalism, a shortcoming that has yet to be resolved to this day.

The Last Spike

Final hammer blow united a nation

JIM BURANT

An iconic image of the Canadian national experience, this photograph is what historian Colin Coates has referred to as "proof of a more widespread, popular desire to commemorate the country's past," by creating a "common sense of destiny" for all Canadians.

Taken at Craigellachie, British Columbia, on the cold morning of November 7, 1885, this photo—which shows Donald Smith, president of the Canadian Pacific Railway, driving the final spike in the railway linking East to West—almost didn't get taken. The photographer, Alexander Ross from Calgary, was probably there only by chance. Another photographer, Cornelius Soule of Toronto, had intended to be at the ceremony, but could not make it in time. Ross would take three separate photographs of the event, of which this has become the most famous.

Although writer and historian Pierre Berton is credited with popularizing the "Last Spike" image, the photograph was actually widely disseminated by the Canadian Pacific Railway within a few years after it was taken. The image would be reproduced countless times in countless formats.

But note the typically Canadian lack of fanfare: neither the prime minister nor his chief political rivals are present. There's no throng of reporters to document the momentous occasion—just Donald Smith, surrounded by some railway staff and a few other luminaries. The spike itself is a modest thing, made out of iron, not the customary gold. All in all, it was a modest event celebrating an unbelievable national achievement.

Think about the accomplishment: The fledgling country of Canada, with a population of 4.3 million people in 1881, had managed to build the longest railway in the world, through some of the worst terrain imaginable, and well ahead of schedule. Financed by British and American capital, it cost the Canadian government 10.4 million hectares of the best prairie land, soaked up an estimated $63.5 million in public funds and $35 million in government loans, and took 12,000 men—mostly immigrant labourers—5,000 horses, and 300 dogsled teams to build. Hundreds of men lost their lives to illness and accidents, and the displacement of Canada's First Nations would also cost the nation in years to come. But as a national achievement, the railway was unprecedented.

In later years, as the West opened up to settlement, and trade and tourism flourished, the railway provided a symbol of technological and political achievement for the country.

The photo itself represents a moment in time, and within a contemporary critical analysis would suffer badly, since it singularly fails to contain any representations of the women, Chinese labourers, and First Nations peoples who also helped to build the railway. The photo's popularity has also waxed and waned, as the strength of Canadian nationalism has fluctuated.

Whether Alexander Ross understood this when he took the photo on that cold November morning is unknown; what he did create, though, was an indelible record of an astounding moment in our national memory.

Donald Smith drives "the Last Spike" at Craigellachie, B.C., November 7, 1885.

9

Looking Chilkoot Pass

Gold-rush miners carrying heavy packs up the steep slopes
of Chilkoot Pass, B.C., circa 1898–99.

The Golden Staircase

Chilkoot Pass tested miners' mettle

TINA LOO

No matter how quickly prospectors made it to Seattle, and then Skagway or Dyea in Alaska, the Coast Mountains ensured there would be no *rush* for Yukon gold in 1897, especially for those who couldn't afford to have their goods packed or hoisted up on a tramway. In its last kilometre, the trail shot up over 300 metres before depositing the stampeders at the top of Chilkoot Pass.

Whatever relief these gold seekers may have felt reaching the summit was fleeting. After stacking their supplies outside the stone house that served as Canadian customs, they went back down to where the balance of their belongings sat and repeated the journey, again and again.

Thanks to the Canadian government, which insisted miners have a year's worth of supplies, the "golden staircase"—1,500 steps cut into the snow and ice—was more like purgatory than a stairway to heaven. To move one outfit, some miners packed and cached their goods up to forty times, sometimes spending three months getting from Dyea to the top of Chilkoot Pass.

Despite the rigours of the trail, the promise of striking it rich, especially in the middle of a global economic downturn, was enough to move people over mountains. There were a number of different ways to get to the goldfields from the Alaska coast, but the Chilkoot Trail, developed by the Tlingit, was the shortest and potentially fastest route.

Fast was a relative term. Although news of the gold strike made it out in August, very few outsiders arrived in Dawson in 1897. Just getting over the pass with their supplies was a monumental accomplishment, but even after doing so the miners were still 800 kilometres from their destination.

Most wintered on the shores of Lake Lindemann and Lake Bennett, in tent cities housing tens of thousands of men who busied themselves building boats for the rollercoaster ride down the Yukon River. At spring breakup in 1898, approximately 7,000 watercraft of various kinds put into its roiling waters.

Hope floats, but time sank the aspirations of many a fortune seeker. After travelling for months, miners arrived in Dawson in the summer only to discover that almost all the claims had been staked by locals. Devastated, some left, but others made the best of it, working for other miners on their claims, slinging beer or food in Dawson's many saloons and restaurants, or packing goods in and out of the goldfields.

The miners climbing the golden staircase are optimism embodied, in all its grunting, aching form. Their story is about hope as much as the limits imposed by body, space, and time. In that sense, this image—an image of an exceptional event—captures something of the timeless spirit and experience of everyone who journeyed to this land to make a better life.

Over (in) a Barrel

Foolhardy stunt inspired countless daredevils

NELLE OOSTEROM

In this picture, a shaken but still standing Annie Edson Taylor is assisted to the Canadian shore on October 24, 1901, after becoming the first person known to have gone over Niagara Falls and lived.

The sixty-three-year-old widow suffered a gash to her head and was in shock, but was otherwise unscathed, after tumbling over the falls in a barrel. Several thousand people witnessed the event, and, as the *New York Times* said, "everybody agreed it was a foolhardy trip."

Taylor was not the first to perform a "foolhardy" stunt at Niagara Falls, nor was she the last. Every since it first became a tourist destination after the war of 1812, the world's second-largest waterfall has had a long-standing relationship with daredevil artists and the gawkers who come out to watch them risk their lives. By 1901, high-wire artists had walked over the falls on tightropes so many times in so many different ways that it had become old hat. The Great Blondin—Jean-François Gravelot—did it first. Over two summer seasons in 1859 and 1860, he not only walked over the falls on a tightrope, he rode a bicycle, pushed a wheelbarrow, and, in one case, carried a man on his back. Many followed the Great Blondin's lead.

With high-wire acts so *yesterday* by the 1880s, aspiring daredevils dreamed up new amazing feats. It was a cooper, appropriately enough, who first conceived the idea of going over the falls in a barrel. In 1886, Carlisle D. Graham was the first to safely navigate the deadly Whirlpool Rapids below the falls, but he never made good on his intention of going over the falls itself. Graham was there to witness Annie Edison Taylor do it, though, and, like many that day, he must have questioned her sanity. Here was a grandmotherly woman in petticoats venturing into the heart of a watery maelstrom where no man had yet dared to go. "My God, she's alive!" Graham reportedly shouted after rescuers retrieved the barrel and found a bedraggled, but still breathing, Taylor inside. In this picture, Graham is the man on the left looking up.

Taylor, with her clothing soaked but her hair still held tight in its bun, is extending her hand to William "Red" Hill Sr., the man in the hat. He went on to become famous for his own daredevilry and his many amazing rescues at the falls.

After her terrifying trip, Taylor declared: "Nobody ought ever to do that again." Yet her stunt only seemed to fuel more fascination with conquering Niagara's unforgiving torrents. Other barrel riders, both women and men, followed her, some with fatal results.

Taylor—a New York–born teacher and dance instructor who had lost her husband during the American Civil War—hoped the stunt would lift her out of poverty. It did not. She died penniless twenty years later. Meanwhile, the staging of death-defying performances at the falls continues well into the new millennium, even though it has long been illegal to do so.

10

Mrs. Annie Edson Taylor, the first person to survive going over Niagara Falls in a barrel, October 24, 1901.

Onondaga distance runner Tom Longboat wins the Boston Marathon, April 19, 1907.

11

The Road Warrior

Fleet young marathoner outran his critics

ANDRÉ PICARD

Marathoners, like cyclists, usually peak in their late twenties to early thirties. So the idea that a young man, barely out of his teens, could win the legendary Boston Marathon is almost unthinkable.

But that is precisely what Tom Longboat did on April 19, 1907. He ran the race in a blistering 2:24:24, shattering the course record by almost five minutes.

The hordes of spectators who braved the cold, rainy weather that day were rewarded with a glimpse of a man in a tattered T-shirt, swim trunks held up by a belt, and flimsy leather shoes—a man the *Boston Globe* dubbed "the most marvellous runner who has ever sped over our roads."

And marvellous Longboat was. Lithe and lean, he ran swiftly and effortlessly. But off the racecourse, the road was much bumpier. As an aboriginal person, Longboat was a second-class citizen and was routinely defamed and exploited. At the height of his fame, he was treated more like a racehorse than a human; Longboat's exploits enriched managers and bettors, but ultimately left him broke and broken.

An Onondaga whose given name was Cogwagee, Longboat was born in a log cabin on the Six Nations reserve near Brantford, Ontario, in 1887. As a young boy, he became a protege of Bill Davis, a gifted Mohawk runner. At the time, Canadians dominated distance running, and the sport was immensely popular, particularly with gamblers.

Longboat made his racing debut on Victoria Day, 1905, and he soon excelled at the sport. However, with world acclaim came controversy. At the 1908 Olympics in London, for instance, Longboat was favoured to win the marathon—but he collapsed and did not finish. One theory holds that Longboat's own backers drugged him and made a small fortune betting against the Canadian marathoner.

Longboat later turned pro and went on to set a raft of world records. Despite his success, he was often described as lazy because he liked to alternate his hard training days with rest, an approach that is now common practice. He was also stereotyped as a "drunken Indian"—smears that emerged from his highly publicized disputes with managers, mostly about money. The *Globe and Mail* summed him up as follows: "Longboat was . . . a fleet genius with a well-bent elbow. He ran and drank and roistered."

Longboat, though, would outrun his critics; his legacy as an inspiration for all Canadians— regardless of race—has lived on long after the naysayers were silenced. During the First World War, he enlisted and worked as a dispatch runner in France, a perilous job. After the war, he took a job with the City of Toronto as a trash collector. He remained there for more than two decades before retiring to the Six Nations reserve.

Longboat died on January 9, 1949, and was buried in a traditional ceremony. A flag draped his coffin, and near its head, in Onondaga tradition, a notch was cut in the shape of a V, allowing his spirit to escape and join his ancestors. There is no doubt he made the journey swiftly.

Rushing Toward Disaster

Bridge collapse a reminder of the cost of hubris

JACQUES LACOURSIÈRE

It was not yet constructed, and already people were calling it the "eighth wonder of the world."

The massive cantilever bridge being built just upriver from Quebec City was to be the largest span of its kind—the latest in a line of engineering marvels, such as Montreal's Victoria Bridge and the Eiffel Tower in Paris, that illustrated the growth in technological prowess around the turn of the nineteenth century. It was 1907, just one year before a planned major celebration of the tricentennial of Quebec City's founding, and everything about the project felt rushed.

For quite some time, there had been a desire to link the south and north shores of the St. Lawrence River near Quebec City. In 1903, the Quebec Bridge Company contracted the job of building the span to the Phoenix Bridge Company of Phoenixville, Pennsylvania. Engineer Theodore Cooper, an American, was given the job of designing it. Construction began in late summer of 1904 on the first anchor arm on the south shore. Work progressed quickly, and soon the cantilevered portion protruded above the waters of the St. Lawrence River.

But at the beginning of February 1906, an on-site engineer expressed concern that the weight of the metal was heavier than anticipated. Cooper, the chief engineer, worked out of a New York City office and had not actually been back to the work site since 1903. He was in his mid-sixties, in poor health, and didn't want to travel. When told of the concerns, Cooper downplayed them; after all, they had a schedule to meet.

Back in Quebec, however, concern was turning to worry. The metal in the bridge was clearly stressed. In late August 1907 a young engineer, Norman McClure—appointed by Cooper himself—decided to travel to New York and to Phoenixville to raise these concerns in person.

But it was too late.

On August 29, 1907, at precisely 5:37 p.m.—just as McClure was entering the Phoenix Bridge Company office in Phoenixville—the south structure of the bridge collapsed with an infernal noise. Tons of steel crashed into the river, taking about one hundred workers with them. Some were crushed beneath twisted metal. Rescue would have to be rapid, as tidal waters threatened to swallow both debris and men. The majority of the injured were in critical condition. All told, seventy-six workers would die in the collapse.

In 1908, a Royal Commission probed the disaster and concluded that there were "errors in judgment" on the part of Cooper and another engineer from the Phoenix Bridge Company, Peter Szlapka.

Construction on a second bridge would begin in 1913. An accident during construction in 1916 claimed the lives of thirteen workers. It would be three more years before the bridge was officially inaugurated by the future King Edward VIII.

This photo is a sombre reminder of the costs of human error; sometimes, there's a steep price to be paid for our failures.

12

Quebec Bridge collapse, one of the worst
disasters of its kind in the world, August 29, 1907.

13

"A Girl from Canada," part of an immigration promotion campaign in England, 1907.

The "Girl from Canada"

Millions of immigrants answered nation's siren call

MICHAEL BLISS

Do you think she could possibly ride that overloaded bicycle? Even if she were wearing more sensible clothes?

The "Girl from Canada," who trotted her bike around Britain in the early years of the twentieth century, does not quite fit female stereotypes of her age. She is not the wispy, ethereal "Miss Canada" usually depicted as needing protection from a leering Uncle Sam. She is not quite hardy enough to be "Janey Canuck," the pants-wearing, sleeves-rolled-up sister to hardy lumberman Johnny Canuck. She is certainly not Kipling's "Our Lady of the Snows," who would be much too wintry and frosty to attract anyone to life in Britain's great North American Dominion.

She looks short and English. She'd probably emigrated a few years earlier, perhaps to the Canadian Prairies, what the Canadian Department of the Interior—which sponsored her immigration recruiting tours—called "the Last Best West." On her homestead—land free for the taking—she evidently produced an abundance of grains, some of which won "First Prize" in agricultural competitions, and she appears to have bought fine woven baskets made by Canadian aboriginals. In 1907, a woman with her own bicycle and wearing a fine, masculine hat implies liberation from farm work. Her full skirts suggest she spends more of her time in the kitchen than in the fields.

If the twentieth century was going to belong to Canada, as Prime Minister Wilfrid Laurier had predicted, the vast country needed to attract millions of new Canadians. A country that still thought of itself as British—that still used Britain's flags—expected most of its newcomers also to be British. The best publicity came from the boys and girls who did well in the New World and came home to tell about it. And so the "Girl from Canada" hit the road, travelling throughout Britain trying to lure the locals across the Atlantic. The tactic must have worked: about one million Britons came out to Canada to try their luck in the two decades before the Second World War.

While it's true that Canada tried hardest to woo English, Irish, and Scots lads and lasses, and shamefully discriminated against non-Caucasians in its immigration policies, the need for people was so great that women and men from other countries were also being courted. As Minister of the Interior Clifford Sifton famously said, Canada welcomed anyone willing to work hard, even peasants who wore sheepskin coats.

There are few pictures of smiling girls who came to Canada from Ruthenia, Galicia, and other areas of Central Europe. Their lives were much too hard. Nor did their homelands welcome Canadian immigration agents or campaigns—especially not campaigns featuring semi-emancipated women and their bicycles.

Wings and a Prayer

First flight lifted Canadians' spirits

CHARLOTTE GRAY

The *Silver Dart*, with its silk wings, tricycle wheels, and bamboo and wire frame, seemed too flimsy a construction to carry a man's weight, let alone establish a record. Yet on February 23, 1909, John McCurdy climbed into the pilot's seat and started the V8 fifty-horsepower engine. Volunteers on skates pushed the flying machine, with its fifteen-metre wingspan and no brakes, along the frozen surface of Bras d'Or Lake, the massive inland sea in Cape Breton. Wobbly at first, the little plane gathered speed and then, to the delight of onlookers, lifted nine metres in the air and flew almost 1.5 kilometres.

Why is this photograph important? Because it was proof—proof that the record for the first controlled powered flight by a British subject in the British Empire had been established. There had been plenty of enthusiastic witnesses from the local fishing village of Baddeck, but no reporters from national newspapers such as Toronto's *Globe* or the *New York Times* had made the three-day journey to the remote corner of Nova Scotia to watch. Nobody, however, could quarrel with this image of soaring wings.

The Aviation Age was just beginning: the Wright Brothers had launched the first powered biplane at Kitty Hawk, North Carolina, in December 1903. But they had refused to publish photographs of their triumph because they feared rivals might steal their innovations.

Rumours of their achievement had captured the imagination of Alexander Graham Bell, who was already obsessed with the idea of manned flight. For years, the Washington-based inventor had been building massive kites and primitive helicopters at his summer estate in Nova Scotia. He and his wife, Mabel, put together the Aerial Experiment Association, a group of four young men working under Bell's direction, with the goal, as one of them put it, of getting "into the air."

The *Silver Dart* was the fourth of the AEA's biplanes (its three predecessors all flew in the United States), each of which included vital improvements in flight controls and landing-gear designs. Bell's successes, and the circulation of photographs like this, contributed to the fizz and thrill of the flying-machine craze, and to public confidence that soon airplanes would be an accessible form of transport.

At a more personal level, this photograph was proof of something else, too. It reassured sixty-two-year-old Alec Bell that his mind was as creative and productive as it had been thirty-three years earlier, when he invented the telephone. The intervening years had been filled with frustrations and failures. As the *Silver Dart* soared off into the white winter sky, Bell's spirits lifted with it.

14

PLAN

of

BEINN BHREAGH

the

CAPE BRETON ESTATE of

Dr A. G. Bell.

Scale 200 to 1

Area — 600 acres

The *Silver Dart* over Baddeck Bay, February 23, 1909.

Would-be immigrants from India detained aboard the *Komagata Maru*, Burrard Inlet, B.C., 1914.

15

The *Komagata Maru*

Image of injustice marks shameful moment in history

CHRISTOPHER MOORE

In May 1914, there was fear and hatred in British Columbia. When the *Komagata Maru* anchored in Vancouver harbour, its passengers encountered both. The fear: that immigrants descending en masse from Asia would change British Columbia from a prosperous British-Canadian society into an outpost of teeming Asia. The hatred: a deep, racist hostility to people denounced by some whites as barbarous, apelike, subhuman, and evil.

For twenty years, a punitive head tax had kept out Chinese immigration. Meanwhile, Japan had been coerced into restricting migration. In 1904, British Columbia's fears revived when workers from India began coming to the province. These, however, were British subjects—entitled by law to move from one part of the empire to another. It seemed nothing could prevent them from immigrating.

In 1907, the Asiatic Exclusion Society whipped up an anti-Sikh riot in Vancouver. Faced with this chaos, the federal government yielded. It issued orders-in-council under the Immigration Act: only Indians who made "one continuous voyage" could be admitted. Then Canada coerced the shipping lines to cancel direct sailings from India.

Sikh leaders quickly determined to test Canada's ban. Entrepreneur Gurdit Singh Sarhali chartered the steamship *Komagata Maru* in Japan and recruited 376 Sikhs and Hindus who were eager to work in Canada. They took heart from recent court decisions in British Columbia that had found the orders-in-council incompatible with the Immigration Act. This would be the test case: in British Canada, did British Indians have the rights of British subjects?

When the *Komagata Maru* reached Vancouver in May 1914, immigration officers harassed the passengers. Troops guarded the docks. The naval cruiser HMCS *Rainbow* added menace. Weeks passed, and the passengers lay trapped aboard ship, hungry, hot, filthy, but defiant—forbidden to land, but refusing to leave without a hearing. Our photographer shows them still smiling, perhaps still confident.

The Sikhs' lawyer wanted to challenge the law in court. "*If* we can find an honest court to go to," the anti-immigrant local MP snarled in reply; the MP feared that the judges would once more rule Canada's too-clever stratagems illegal. In the end, Munshi Singh, a twenty-six-year-old farmer, became the test case. The immigration board ordered him deported, and his appeal went swiftly to five judges of the province's highest court. Earlier in 1914, Canada had amended its orders-in-council so that they no longer blatantly contradicted the Immigration Act. Would the reworded orders-in-council stand up in court? Yes, they would. The court said that the clearly expressed will of Parliament cancelled the timeless rights of British subjects.

HMCS *Rainbow* escorted the *Komagata Maru* out to sea, and the would-be immigrants went bitterly back to India. South Asian immigration would not pick up again until the 1950s.

Today, one million South Asian Canadians have overcome the hate, disproved the fears, and become valued and productive members of multicultural Canada. In 2008, Canada formally acknowledged the injustice done in 1914.

The Boy and the Bear

16

Beloved Pooh Bear inspired by Canadian cub

DEBORAH MORRISON

One of the world's classic literary characters began simply, as all good children's stories do. On a crisp August morning in 1914, a train carrying Harry Colebourn, a young veterinarian and lieutenant of the 34th Fort Garry Horse and Canadian Army Veterinary Corps, pulled up to a routine stop in White River, Ontario. When the train stopped, Colebourn spied a trapper with a black bear cub leashed beside him.

The trapper had killed its mother, and knew that the cub would not survive on its own in the forest, so he brought it into the town in the hopes of selling it as a pet. Harry Colebourn paid the trapper twenty dollars for the bear and named her "Winnie" after his hometown of Winnipeg.

Like so many Canadian men, Colebourn had enlisted to fight in the Great War and was en route to Valcartier, Quebec, where the Canadian Expeditionary Force was gathering. He believed that Winnie could prove to be a source of entertainment and good cheer for the regiment, and he was not disappointed. She travelled with them overseas to Salisbury Plain, England—where this charming photograph was taken—and stayed with them for the next eight weeks until the unit was called over to France in December 1914.

During this time, Winnie quickly became a beloved mascot. Soldiers played with her during their off hours. She was frequently chased out of tents, where she was often caught shimmying up the centre pole. Each night, she slept inside the tent under Colebourn's cot.

With every intention of returning for Winnie when the war was over, Colebourn negotiated a temporary home for her at the London Zoo. Even as she grew into an adult bear, Winnie was remarkably tame and friendly. Consequently, she became a star attraction at the zoo for Londoners looking for moments of pleasure and wonder among the grim realities of wartime life.

Among them was Christopher Robin, the son of children's author A.A. Milne. This chance meeting between boy and bear would inspire Milne to create a collection of tales about a honey-loving little bear and his menagerie of talking animal pals (themselves inspired by the stuffed animals in young Christopher Robin's room).

How many countless children have since thrilled to the tales of Winnie-the-Pooh, Piglet, Rabbit, and Roo? And how many untold millions of dollars has the Winnie-the-Pooh cottage industry of films, books, T-shirts, and toys generated?

Colebourn, of course, had no idea in 1914 what the future held for his beloved Winnie. He and his unit were part of the first Canadian contingent, numbering 33,000, which went to England soon after the outbreak of war in 1914. By the end of the war, the contributions of the Canadian Expeditionary Force would earn them international respect and help establish Canada's independence from Britain.

Winnie would establish a reputation of her own, and Colebourn would donate her permanently to the London Zoo, where, up until the time of her death in 1927, her presence would serve as another reminder of Canada's unique contributions and connections to England.

POST CARD

CARTE POSTALE
Address—Adresse

STAMP
HERE

Winnie the Bear with Canadian soldier
Harry Colebourn, Salisbury Plain, England, 1914.

On the back of this photograph
Great Grandfather had written, "Myse
Winnie, the Bear. Winnie is now on
at the Zoo in London but is coming bac
Canada with me someday. Kind Regards
'Arry! "

17

Over the Top, a training exercise near St. Pol, France, 1916.

Over the Top

Iconic war image not what it seems

TIM COOK

This is the most famous photograph of Canadians in the Great War. It captures the infantry on the firing line and ready to "go over the top" to cross the killing fields of no man's land, where shot and shell will leave soldiers torn and shattered. This evocative image captures the anxiety before battle and the unknowingness of soldiers who are about to face death.

It's also a fake.

The Great War was the most traumatic event in Canadian history. By war's end, some 20 percent of all males had served overseas, and some 66,000 had been killed. It was a war that was reported on daily. Photographs were important in keeping Canadians abreast of the situation overseas, and to keep up spirits.

Sir Max Aitken—later Lord Beaverbrook, an expatriate multi-millionaire—was responsible for publicizing Canada's overseas war effort. Beaverbrook used his powerful connections and nearly limitless funds to break the War Office's objections to having photographers at the front. By the summer of 1916, Beaverbrook had arranged for official photographers, filmmakers, and artists to document the Canadians at the front.

But taking photographs at the sharp end of the conflict was difficult. The equipment was fragile and bulky. Snipers' bullets, shrapnel, and high explosives discouraged photographers from raising their heads or cameras above the trench parapets. When they did, the smoke and explosions made it difficult to get any useful shots of Canadians in combat.

Official photographer William Ivor Castle had a solution. He would photograph the Canadians behind the lines. He and other photographers also employed darkroom techniques to add in shellfire bursts above soldiers.

This image, shot at a training camp at St. Pol, France, was passed off as a true representation of soldiers in the front lines ready for battle. But does it matter that the soldiers here were not at the front? Does it lose any of its power in capturing the essence of battle when we know that it was taken in a training area rather than on the killing ground of the Western Front? Do photographs have to represent the *truth*?

Most observers would say yes, assuming a photograph is a truthful and accurate representation of something that happened, and is captured through the photographic process. Yet what about events that fall outside the lens's view, remaining undocumented by choice? If we allow that art can capture the essence of an event, person, or place, is there no room for this in photographs?

What happens when a photograph this evocative represents an imagined event better than any truthful representation?

Hats Off to Victory

18

Feisty feminists celebrated right to vote in style

CHARLOTTE GRAY

They don't look much like revolutionaries, do they? Yet these three women, with their motherly expressions and sensible coats, had just scored a major political victory. A few hours earlier, on April 19, 1916, the Alberta legislature had passed a bill granting women the right to vote in provincial elections.

The suffrage effort was a team effort—and what a team! Alice Jamieson, in the centre, kick-started the Alberta suffrage campaign in 1910 when she headed the local Council of Women. She was joined by Emily Murphy, on the right, a popular prairie writer and bulldozer of a woman, with a loud laugh, iron will, and, according to a contemporary, "the lusty seagoing roll of a sailor." Best known of this trio is the redoubtable Nellie McClung, on the left. McClung had been a leader in the suffrage campaign in Manitoba (which in January 1916 had become the first province to give women the vote), but had moved to Alberta in 1914.

These women all faced a great deal of old-fashioned sexism in their public lives. In Britain and the United States, first-wave feminists often responded with anger or violence. But "Our Nell," as she was widely known, trademarked a typically Canadian response: satire. She once wrote, "I wish you could see the proportion of my mail that tells me to go home and darn my husband's socks. I never would have believed one man's hosiery could excite the amount of interest those socks do!"

Today, McClung's mumsy mix of traditional expectation and radical ideas seems hokey, but in her own era it allowed her to get through her audience's defences.

On the day the Alberta bill passed, McClung and her two Alberta comrades watched the proceedings, then emerged triumphantly from the legislature onto Edmonton's Jasper Avenue. Champagne was out of the question because McClung was an ardent temperance advocate (the temperance movement drew her into politics in the first place). Then the women spied a millinery shop, and Murphy let out a whoop. Look at the hats they chose! Jamieson's dignified bonnet with velvet fur below. Emily's feathered cloche, which smacks of a military helmet. And McClung's jaunty wide-brimmed affair, with an enormous artificial flower softening its crisp lines. This photograph captures the combination of middle-class respectability and don't-mess-with-me glee that so discomfited their critics.

By 1922, six more provinces and the federal government had granted women the right to vote. But the women in this photo were still hell-bent on changing Canada and winning gender equality. In 1929, Emily Murphy and Nellie McClung went on to lead the legal battle for women to be considered "persons" under the law, and therefore eligible to be appointed to the Senate. Neither Murphy nor McClung was appointed to the Senate, however; despite those Sunday best hats, they were just too damn mouthy.

If they were alive today, they would likely still be fighting for equality. As McClung herself once said, "The end is not yet!"

From left, Nellie McClung, Alice Jamieson, and Emily Murphy in Edmonton, April 19, 1916.

O.1405

Jubilant Canadian soldiers returning from victory at Vimy Ridge, April 1917.

Vimy's Victors

Famous fight filled Canadians with pride

PETER MANSBRIDGE

These men should be happy. They survived the Battle of Vimy Ridge.

For the first time in the Great War, all four Canadian divisions had fought together, and they had succeeded in pushing the Germans off the fourteen-kilometre-long ridge, which was strategically important because it dominated a huge area of flat land. They had succeeded where the French and British had failed time and time again.

The Germans had held the ridge since 1914 and were securely dug in. At 5:30 in the morning on April 9, 1917—Easter Monday—the Canadians started to take it back. The weather was awful. There was a mixture of sleet and snow, and a biting wind. Incredibly, the Canadians captured almost every objective in less than seven hours. They would push on to complete victory by April 12.

The Canadians had prepared for the battle for months, and they had used a new tactic, the "creeping barrage" of artillery fire, to perfection. The men had advanced behind a deafening curtain of exploding shells, moving forward at a steady, predetermined pace. But they had also needed grim determination and acts of individual heroism. Four men were awarded Victoria Crosses at Vimy, the highest military medal of valour. Two of the medals were awarded posthumously.

They were two of the 3,598 Canadians killed. Another 7,004 Canadians were wounded. On the German side, there were 20,000 casualties. These are astounding numbers to us today, but in that monstrous war, that rate of death was routine.

So yes, these men, returning from Vimy, should be happy—if only because they survived. But there's more going on here.

First, you can tell that the men have had at least a little time to recover from the sheer exhaustion of battle. They're all freshly shaven and clean. Like most battles of the First World War, the fight at Vimy Ridge was carried out in mud that was often knee-deep. And the men have clearly spotted the photographer. They obviously weren't rolling through France waving and smiling as they bounced along every kilometre of dirt road. You can see the soldier on the ground, turning to see what everyone else is looking at. The truck just ahead is quiet. Those men have passed the photographer.

The picture, then, captures Canadians who want to exhibit their confidence and pride. They know they have achieved what seemed impossible. Their spirit was reflected in Canada, where a country just fifty years old was able, for the first time, to feel special as a nation, not as part of an empire.

When the war ended, the Canadian government felt justified in demanding a separate place at the peace table. Our soldiers had fought as Canadians, and we would sign the Treaty of Versailles as Canadians.

The Halifax Explosion

Survivors' resilience inspired Canadians

KEN McGOOGAN

One of the women carries a basket. The other three carry light bundles—a few items salvaged, one might think, from the destruction around them. Closer inspection suggests a different scenario. The picture, taken by Toronto photographer William James, is entitled "Women walking in area destroyed by Halifax Explosion." It is dated December 1917.

The infamous blast occurred in Halifax Harbour on December 6. A French vessel loaded with munitions, the *Mont Blanc*, collided with a Belgian relief ship, the *Imo*. The French ship caught fire, and for twenty minutes a few heroic sailors fought to extinguish the blaze.

When the *Mont Blanc* exploded, it devastated five square kilometres, reducing neighbourhoods to the rubble we see here. Black smoke whirled skyward, and then burning oil and hot metal rained down. A tsunami several metres high crashed over the waterfront and roared through the city streets. More than two thousand people died. Nearly 10,000 were injured, many of them severely burned, and 6,000 instantly were homeless.

The blast was the largest man-made explosion to date. Decades later, during the Second World War, nuclear physicist J. Robert Oppenheimer would study the Halifax Explosion to anticipate the effects of nuclear weapons.

And yet, to analyze this frozen moment today, more than one hundred years after it happened, is to discover a message of hope. This is a photograph of life after death, of dogged persistence, of rebirth and renewal.

It must have been taken about a week after the blast. Fires continue to smoulder, judging from the plumes of smoke we see in the distance, but the roads have been cleared of debris, and James would have needed time to reach Halifax from Toronto.

The four women are survivors. If they have suffered personal loss and trauma, they nonetheless march stoically along the open road.

Perhaps the women have retrieved what they could from ruined homes. But at this time, the vast majority of black Haligonians lived in Africville, a modest community built around a wooden church, a school, and three stores. Most of its residents worked for the railroad or in the dockyards. While badly damaged—doors blown off, windows shattered—Africville remained standing and suffered less destruction than areas closer to the harbour.

Perhaps those buildings in the distance mark the near edge of Africville. Certainly, because they walk with such purpose, these women could be heading off to work. And as they stride towards a blasted area where they are desperately needed, they carry lunch and personal effects.

Already, we see, they have covered some distance. Having survived the devastation that surrounds them, they march determinedly into the future to become, at this remove, symbols of hope and renewal, and of the indestructibility of the human spirit.

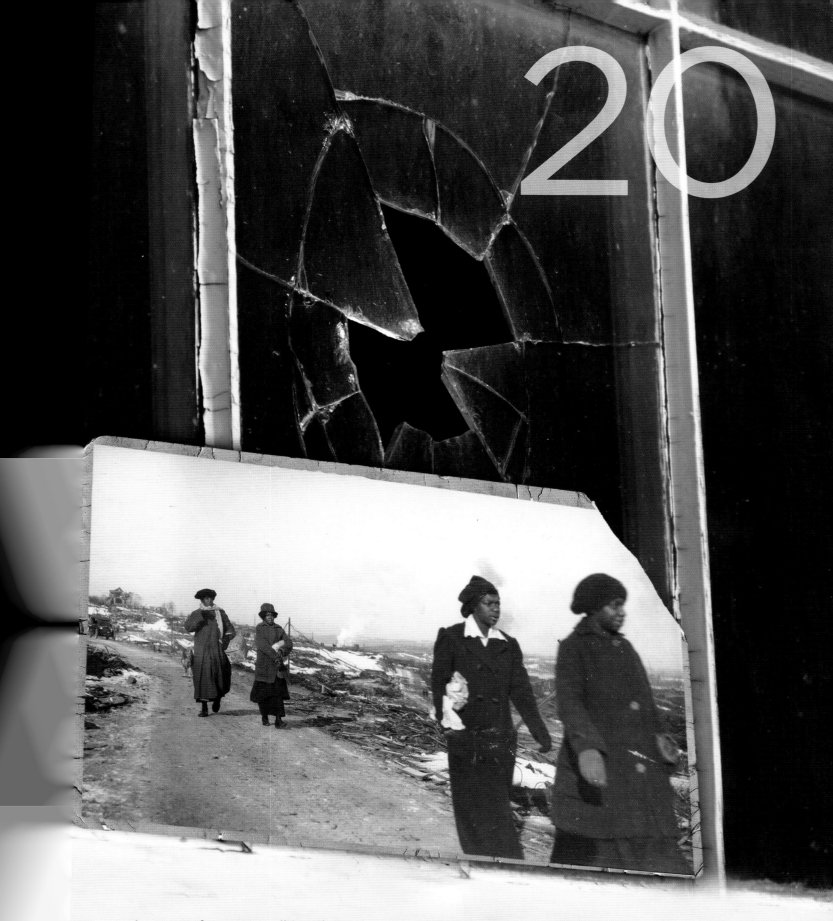

A group of women walking through Halifax following the explosion, December 1917.

Alberta telephone service workers masked against the deadly Spanish flu virus, 1918.

The Spanish Flu

"Perfect storm" pandemic panicked Canadians

ANDRÉ PICARD

Influenza, a seemingly innocuous virus, is actually a mass killer. The virus mutates constantly, and when social, environmental, and biological factors converge just so, it can be particularly lethal.

This "perfect storm" occurred at the end of the First World War, when the Spanish flu wreaked havoc around the world and panicked war-weary Canadians. The pandemic killed somewhere between 25 million and 100 million people around the globe (some researchers believe vast numbers of deaths in the developing world went unrecorded), including some 50,000 in Canada. Far more died of the Great Influenza than did in the bloody Great War that preceded it.

In this photo, a group of Alberta telephone service workers can be seen outside their offices in the fall of 1918. What is striking is the casual eeriness of the pose. Fear of the Spanish flu was such that wearing surgical masks became the social norm—even for telephone operators. It was almost mandatory, as people were refused access to public facilities like buses, stores, and banks unless they wore a mask designed to limit the spread of germs. Many communities banned public gatherings and, in some places, shaking hands became a criminal offence.

But there were families to feed and there was work to be done. One can only guess what the four women from the telephone company are thinking, but there can be little doubt they are not smiling behind the masks. In their eyes, you see fear and consternation.

In the reflection of the store window there is a grain elevator, just beside the railway tracks. One of the main reasons that Spanish flu was so deadly was the unprecedented mass movement of people around the world during and after the war.

Battlefield trenches were perfect incubators for illness, as were crowded boats returning from Europe. Then soldiers and their family members gathered for Armistice celebrations and fanned out across the country. Modern transportation systems made it easy for the disease to spread quickly. Not even the most remote Arctic communities were spared. Depleted resources in the postwar era left little money for public health programs that could have slowed the spread of the disease, and hospitals were already overwhelmed dealing with the war wounded. Worse, there were few effective treatments for the unusually gruesome symptoms—such as horrific coughing and bleeding from the ears—leaving the infected to suffer terribly.

Communities were under siege from an invisible enemy. The flu usually harms the most vulnerable: the very young and the elderly. But the Spanish flu hit particularly hard in the twenty-to-forty age group—the parents and wage-earners in society. Women like those in this photo were most at risk, yet they soldiered on, just as the troops had done.

And if this image seems like a scene from another time and place, consider that in 2003 some Torontonians donned surgical masks, gripped by fear over a SARS virus outbreak. History repeating itself, indeed.

Strife on the Streets

Strikers dealt blow for workers' rights

J.L GRANATSTEIN

The Great War's end found Canada under stress. The fighting had resulted in a huge number of dead and wounded soldiers. Canada's veterans, meanwhile, were expecting to be quickly reintegrated into the domestic economy. The trouble was, the economy was suffering, with munitions factories shutting down and galloping inflation. There were still tensions between French- and English-speaking Canadians over conscription and many veterans saw farmers and profiteers and all others who had stayed home as slackers.

The pot boiled over in Winnipeg in May and June 1919. A dispute over the right to bargain collectively to secure a "living wage" in the metal and building trades galvanized the workers in the Manitoba capital. Soon postmen, firemen, streetcar drivers, telephone operators, civic employees, and power, water, and railway workers walked off the job, and Canada's first major general strike was underway. A Central Strike Committee ran the operation. By mid-May, up to 35,000 men and women were on strike in a city of 175,000.

To the frightened middle and upper class of the city, this was Bolshevism, anarchy, and revolution. A Citizens' Committee sprang into being to represent constituted order and to denounce the "alien scum" who, in its view, controlled the strikers. The city fired its striking employees on May 4 and sacked the police who refused to sign a "no strike" pledge on June 9; 1,800 special constables provided by the Citizens' Committee took over policing.

The federal government stepped in, ordering strikers back to work. It also broadened the definition of sedition and amended the Immigration Act to permit deportation of British subjects—no coincidence, as many strike leaders were British-born.

On June 17, the federal government authorized the arrest of ten strike leaders. Four days later, strikers rallied in Market Square and, as shown in this famous photograph, tried to topple a streetcar operated by strikebreakers. When that failed, they set it on fire. Soon, men of the Royal North West Mounted Police charged on horseback, swinging truncheons. When a Mountie was pulled off his horse and beaten, the officers opened fire on the crowd. More than thirty lay injured after the fracas, with one dead and another dying. Heavily armed militia moved in to take control of the streets. "Bloody Saturday," the strikers called it, and the Strike Committee, alarmed at the police violence, called off the general strike on June 25.

A Royal Commission investigated the affair and criminal trials of the leaders followed. The Commission found many of the workers' grievances justified—but not before most of the arrested strike leaders were jailed and some deported.

The workers would have their revenge, however. In the 1920 Manitoba provincial election, eleven Labour candidates won seats—four of them strike leaders. The next year, Reverend J.S. Woodsworth, one of the strike organizers, won a seat in Parliament. Meanwhile, Arthur Meighen—the acting justice minister who had taken charge of the federal response to the strike, and who was, in 1921, the prime minister—was driven from power in a rout.

22

Protesters overturning a streetcar during the Winnipeg General Strike, June 21, 1919.

23

Members of the Group of Seven
at the Arts and Letters Club, Toronto, 1920

Brushstrokes of History

Artists offered new vision of Canada

MICHAEL BLISS

Canada's most famous "school" of painters never took—or painted—a complete group picture. This sole existing photograph of most members of the Group of Seven is still short one member. From left to right are artists Fred Varley, A.Y. Jackson, Lawren Harris, professor Barker Fairley (a friend and supporter of the group), and artists Frank Johnston, Arthur Lismer, and J.E.H. MacDonald. The absent seventh member of the group was Frank Carmichael.

The group was formed in 1919 to hold joint exhibitions of members' works. Their bold portrayal of the Canadian landscape, applying techniques adapted mainly from European impressionist art, quickly received national and international acclaim. The vagaries of critical fashion have never really dimmed the group's lustre, as its members' best work still ranks among the most sought-after, familiar, and valued of Canadian works of art. You won't find many clues to the group's success in the faces in this picture; instead, you should look at their paintings.

There is a good reason why this picture may convey the impression of the gathering of members of a men's club. It was taken at a 1920 lunch at Toronto's Arts and Letters Club, to which all the members of the group belonged.

So, in fact, did their fiercest critics, such as journalist H.M. Gadsby, who ranted against the "hot mush" school of Canadian painting. Painters and their friends and patrons commonly sat at the "group" table. Scoffers dined at the "knocker's table." Feuds about artistic technique were never allowed to overwhelm the fellowship of men (sorry, no women in either the group or the club) devoted to promoting Canadian art and culture. And, of course, good taste required the wearing of jackets and ties at almost all times. The vaguely bohemian, avant-garde aura of the Arts and Letters Club was wreathed in conservatism and pipe smoke.

Possibly the most talented of this generation of Toronto artists had been Tom Thomson— never a member of either the Group of Seven or the Arts and Letters Club, largely because he was the most solitary outdoorsman of all the painters. In 1917, Thomson had been found dead under mysterious circumstances in Canoe Lake in Algonquin Park. Later in the 1920s, another Toronto painter, A.J. Casson, was welcomed as an eighth member of the Group of Seven. Well into the 1980s, "Cass" would preside at Arts and Letters Club events devoted to anecdotes about the group and the perpetuation of its memory and style. The knocker's table had long since disappeared.

Nanook of the North

Controversial documentary opened eyes to Arctic life

KEN McGOOGAN

An Inuit hunter teaches a boy how to use a bow and arrow. Dressed in traditional fur clothing, he sits on an ice block in front of an igloo, delighting in the boy's progress. The photogenic youth stares directly into the camera, analytical, unafraid. He has what today we might call attitude, and you feel that in adulthood he will be able to size up a charging wolf with the same composure.

The image comes from *Nanook of the North*, a groundbreaking, yet controversial documentary film shot in Inukjuak, northern Quebec, in 1920–21. Hailed as the world's first full-length documentary, *Nanook* accurately portrayed traditional Inuit methods of hunting, fishing and igloo-building. Working without precedent, filmmaker Robert Flaherty—who had prospected and explored in the area—created a loose narrative structure that, in addition to opening and closing sequences, included seven episodes. This photo is a still from episode six, when Nanook, played by a local man named Allakariallak, teaches his supposed son, a boy named Phillipoosie, how to hunt.

The film premiered in New York in June 1922, and overnight became an international sensation. It inspired songs, German ice cream bars, and laudatory books, many of which hailed Flaherty as "the father of the documentary." Almost from inception, *Nanook* elicited praise for its innovative cinematography. In 1989, the American Library of Congress chose *Nanook* as one the first twenty-five films to be preserved in a National Film Registry as "culturally, historically, or aesthetically significant."

Down through the decades, critics have complained that Flaherty distorted reality by hiring actors and staging events. By the 1920s, most Inuit hunters used guns, for example, yet Flaherty portrayed them using ancestral methods and technologies. He argued that a filmmaker must employ artifice to capture the truth of a given subject.

In the 1990s, some academics mounted an ideological attack on explorers and their works. With *Nanook*, they suggested, Flaherty was validating "a colonizing, racist construction of North that constitutes a white American masculinist semiotic of exploration." Such carping blames Flaherty for belonging to the times in which he lived, yet fails to situate the man's accomplishment within its historical context. Contemporary viewers might label *Nanook* a docudrama rather than a documentary, yet the film remains a pioneering work.

In the past couple of years, an Inuit woman named Meeka Mike, a hunter and amateur filmmaker born in the 1960s, has been recording the traditional knowledge of Inuit elders in the South Baffin region of the Arctic. Mike's ambitious project, *Tusaqtuut*, will be far more exhaustive and authentic than Flaherty's seminal film—but then, he was working almost ninety years ago, before Mike's father, now an Inuit elder, had even been born.

Within the constraints of his times, Robert Flaherty strove to transmit traditional Inuit knowledge. *Nanook* points the way to *Tusaqtuut*. Look again at this photo. It represents an extraordinary achievement.

A scene from the film *Nanook of the North*, shot in Inukjuak
(formerly Port Harrison, Northwest Territories), 1921.

PART TWO

A scene from the film *Nanook of the North,* shot in Inukjuak
(formerly Port Harrison, Northwest Territories), 1921.

The *Bluenose*, the fastest schooner in the world, 1921.

25

Sailing into History

Champion schooner set Canadian hearts racing

MARGARET CONRAD

The contest was no nail-biter. On October 24, 1921, Captain Angus Walters and the crew of the *Bluenose* bested their American rival in the race for the International Fishermen's Trophy by a whopping 4.8 kilometres. As newspapers flashed images of the schooner crossing the finish line, the *Bluenose* emerged overnight as a potent—and, all agreed, a beautifully designed—national symbol.

Grand Banks fishermen from Lunenburg, Nova Scotia, and Gloucester, Massachusetts, had long competed with each other for the biggest catch and fastest times to and from port, but the era of wooden sailing ships, even in the fisheries, was fast coming to an end when the *Bluenose* emerged on the scene. Launched on March 26, 1921, the *Bluenose* was less a throwback to the age of sail than an inaugural symbol of the era of mass consumer culture that characterized the interwar years from 1919 to 1939.

The elegant schooner was built in Lunenburg especially to win the International Fishermen's Race, an event initiated by Halifax newspaper owner William H. Dennis, who understood the value of a good news story. Although the *Bluenose* was a working schooner—and took the record for the largest Grand Banks catch in 1923—it was as five-time winner of the international racing series that it gained immortality.

The first race, held in 1920, ended with the Americans defeating the Canadian entry. Dennis and his corporate friends decided to build a new schooner that could win back the Fishermen's Cup. They turned to local ship designer William J. Roué, the Lunenburg shipbuilding firm of Smith & Rhuland, and Captain Angus Walters to achieve their goal. Investing $35,000 in the venture—twice the cost of a regular schooner—they chose the name *Bluenose*, a term used on the Atlantic coast since the eighteenth century to refer to Nova Scotians. No one knows exactly why the *Bluenose* was so successful, but the skill and bull-headedness of Captain Walters no doubt had much to do with it.

The *Bluenose* caught people's imagination throughout Canada and the United States. When the aging vessel sailed in the last of the racing series in 1938, crewmember Doug Pyke took a bag of Canadian dimes, which he sold in the United States for two dollars each as "genuine silver engravings of the *Bluenose*." The previous year, a "Fishing Schooner under Full Sail" had appeared on the Canadian ten-cent piece, and such was the schooner's fame that everyone assumed at the time—and they still do—that it represented the *Bluenose*.

The *Bluenose* spent its final years as a tramp schooner in the Caribbean before sinking off the coast of Haiti in 1946. In 1963, a replica appeared in the form of *Bluenose II*, again sponsored by corporate interests, this time Oland Breweries. *Bluenose II* was sold to the Nova Scotia government in 1971 for a token one dollar, and thereafter has served as an ambassador for the province, as well as a reminder of the happy marriage of capitalism and culture in the interwar years.

PART TWO

FORGED IN FIRE

1922–1955

After four terrible years in the trenches, we wanted to live. The twenties saw hemlines rise and inhibitions fall. We did the Charleston, and despite Prohibition we managed to keep the taps flowing. It wasn't all a party, though. There was growing anger on the streets over a lack of jobs and government support.

Canada had entered the First World War as a junior partner, but departed a peer to the great nations of the world. Our victories on the battle-fields had filled us with a new confidence in our vast Dominion. But as we entered the 1930s, dust clouds loomed over the Prairies, even as darker clouds gathered over Europe. The dirty thirties would prove to be trying times for most Canadians.

All the while, we were taking aboriginal children away from their communities for what was then called "aggressive assimilation"—planting the seeds of a century's worth of tragedy.

When war erupted in Europe in 1939, Canadians grabbed their kits and answered the call. Missing in action, though, was the naive jingoism that had marked our previous march to battle in 1914. Men and women found their lives turned upside down as they trained either for war or for work in the factories.

Meanwhile, Hitler's blitzkrieg carried the Nazis all the way to Paris. Would London be the next to fall? In the fear-filled days of 1941, Canada and its allies needed a hero. They got one, thanks in part to an Ottawa photographer who—with a click of his camera—transformed Britain's cigar-chomping prime minister into a "Roaring Lion."

As the decade progressed, cameras grew more portable. Technologies improved and photography became a crucial tool for the military, both for surveillance and for propaganda campaigns. War photographers patrolled the front lines shooting scenes of heroism to send back to the home front. Soldiers carried snapshots of loved ones into battle like totems.

Canadians greeted the war's end with jubilation, but also with sadness. For the second time in barely thirty years, we had sent our young men away, with many never to return. Back home, the women who had kept the war machine humming suddenly found it tough to trade in their tools for an apron. Yet, as the fifties gleamed on the horizon, spirits were high.

In the postwar euphoria, the baby boom began. As the world splintered along lines of democracy and communism, urbanites in Canada began their march to the suburbs. A car in every driveway, a television in every home, and jobs aplenty—this was the new national dream.

—Mark Reid

26

Schoolchildren dressed in European finery spell out the word "goodbye" at the Fort Simpson Indian Residential School, Northwest Territories, 1922.

86-22-M

Harsh Lessons

Residential school scars run deep

WINONA WHEELER

The title of this photograph is "Indian children holding letters that spell 'Goodbye' at Fort Simpson Indian Residential School." Who or what they were saying farewell to is unknown, but, given what we now know about their experiences, an analogous message could easily be "Goodbye to freedom, culture, language, innocence, pride, normalcy, safety, home, and family."

Between 1831 and 1998, 130 boarding, industrial, and residential schools were funded by the federal government and managed by the Anglican, Methodist, Presbyterian, Roman Catholic, and United churches across Canada. This 1922 photo shows Deh Cho Dene (South Slavey) children at the Fort Simpson Residential School in a village named Liidlii Kue, "the place where the rivers come together" in the Northwest Territories.

Catholic missionaries opened this school in 1920. That same year, the Indian Act was amended, making it mandatory for every Indian child between the ages of seven and fifteen to attend school, on threat of summary conviction for non-compliance. In effect, the federal government took away the rights of parents to raise their own children. It was thought that Indian children had to be isolated from the "backward" cultural influences of their families and immersed in the "civilizing" effects of church and school if there was any hope for eventual assimilation.

Government policy of the time encouraged the public to see Indians as little more than children, incapable of taking on the responsibilities of adulthood, and occupying the lowest rung in society. At the same time, the general public needed assurance that Indians were no longer a threat.

This image—of Indian children in European clothes and haircuts—implicitly and explicitly conveys the message that traditional First Nations cultures are dead, First Nations resistance has ended, and "progress" moves forward. Today, this photo, along with others like it, is a tragic reminder of a shameful and painful period in Canadian history.

Housed in poorly built and maintained dormitories, young children faced appalling living conditions, poor health conditions, and a range of horrific physical and emotional abuses. The year this photograph was taken, Dr. P. H. Bryce, medical inspector for Indian Affairs, published a scathing report on residential schools entitled *The Story of a National Crime*. His recommendations to improve conditions were ignored, and it is estimated that thousands of children died from a variety of illnesses resulting from conditions and treatment at those schools.

The long-term and intergenerational impact of the residential schools is evident in the current socio-economic conditions many First Nations people face. Public awareness, along with apologies from churches and the state, and compensation packages to former inmates, have helped the healing process—but the scars are deep, and the healing journey is still in progress.

Leaping the Gender Gap

Canadian women made great strides at the '28 Games

BY RICHARD W. POUND

Thirty-two years after the revival of the Olympic Games, the all-male International Olympic Committee reluctantly, with the equally reluctant concurrence of the International Amateur Athletic Federation, allowed women to participate in track and field at the 1928 Games in Amsterdam—temporarily putting to one side its uninformed concern that such events would be too strenuous for the "weaker sex."

Onto the scene came the Matchless Six, the Canadian women's team, consisting of high jumper Ethel Catherwood and sprinters Myrtle Cook, Fanny (Bobbie) Rosenfeld, Ethel Smith, Jenny (Jean) Thompson, and Florence Jane Bell. They proved to be the most successful women's athletics team at the '28 Games.

Catherwood—dubbed the Saskatoon Lily—attracted the attention of photographers and spectators alike for the combination of her ability and exceptional beauty.

The Olympic champion in the high jump event, Catherwood was the only athlete to clear 1.59 metres. It was a remarkable accomplishment considering the rules of the day, which prevented even the so-called western roll, much less the complete reverse technique now permitted, which enables female jumpers to clear more than two metres. Catherwood, in the course of a three-hour competition, did not even take off her sweatsuit until the bar was raised to 1.52 metres. Observers said that before each jump, she simply faced the bar, smiled, and then cleared the height.

In addition to the Catherwood gold in high jump, the women's team also won gold in the 4 x 100-metre relay and silver and bronze in the 100-metre sprint. Thompson, who had been expected to win gold in the 800-metre event, finished a disappointing fourth due to an injured leg.

The latter event was a cause for the old men of the IOC and the IAAF to wrap themselves in concern after some of the competitors appeared exhausted and were given minor medical aid at the end of the race. The Belgian IOC president of the day, Count Baillet-Latour, went so far as to suggest that all women's events be removed from the Games. Fortunately, this paternalistic idea was not taken up, but the IAAF did intervene to exclude all races longer than 200 metres for another thirty-two years.

The return to Canada of the Matchless Six following the Games was a triumph, with tickertape parades in both Montreal and Toronto. When Catherwood arrived in Saskatoon, she was greeted by a celebration not seen since the end of the First World War, and was given an educational trust fund to enable her to continue her studies in piano.

The Matchless Six were the example and forerunners for many of Canada's finest Olympic performances, proving over and over again that women cede nothing to men when it comes to international competition.

27

Ethel Catherwood clears 1.59 metres and takes home the gold at the 1928 Summer Olympics in Amsterdam.

28

A man kneels in the dusty landscape of Alberta during the 1930s.

Despair in the Dust Bowl

Dreams were dashed during the dirty thirties

MICHAEL BLISS

Nineteenth-century maps had labelled the prairie lands of the Midwest as "the Great American Desert."

In 1863, explorer John Palliser had warned that the southern regions of what is now eastern Alberta and western Saskatchewan were too arid to ever be opened for agricultural settlement. It happened anyway, in the limitless optimism of the early twentieth century. Several decades of above-average precipitation, combined with record prices for grain, especially during the First World War, had stripped away inhibitions about encouraging settlement in "Palliser's Triangle." Homesteaders had flowed onto the land.

At first they did well. After all, it was the "Last Best West," a land of hope and promise.

Then the climate changed again, reverting to the norm and worse. In the late 1920s and throughout the 1930s, most of the North American Midwest suffered from repeated droughts, plus unusually cold winters and sizzling hot summers. Dry dirt rose up and blew and drifted like snow. Windy weather generated fierce dust storms all over the Great Plains. You could not drive a car in the country, or hold a fair, or play a game of baseball, or even see the barn from your farmhouse window. In this undated picture of an Alberta landscape, all we see is dirt and a poor human victim.

Farmers who had their crops destroyed by drought—or by the ravenous clouds of grasshoppers—were wiped out. Total grain production in Western Canada shrank absolutely during the 1930s. But the cruel paradox of the Great Depression was that the price of grain fell so low—lower than it had been in recorded history—that even in good weather, with a bumper crop, a family still could not make enough money to be able to afford to keep their homestead. So there was more than one reason for the decade's nickname, the dirty thirties.

In the long term, much of the land would be reclaimed by modern conservation techniques, including tree-planting, irrigation, and crop rotation. In the short term, there was nothing to do but leave. The "Okies" of John Steinbeck's novels migrated to California. The dust bowl farmers of Alberta and Saskatchewan, at least a quarter-million of them, moved on to the more stable northern prairies and parkland, or left for British Columbia. Those who stayed lobbied hard for crop insurance, social assistance, and anything to help make it rain.

The human cost of excessive optimism—about the climate, the land, and the future—had been very high.

The Mad Trapper

Mysterious fugitive continues to haunt Canadians

WILL FERGUSON

Consider it a Rorschach test. When you look at the face in the photograph what do you see? A madman? A murderer? Or do you see a tormented soul? A lonely death? The Mad Trapper of Rat River remains a blank canvas even now.

Just about the only thing we know about him for certain is that his name was not Albert Johnson; that was given to him early on and in error.

They called it the "Arctic Circle War," a forty-eight-day pursuit through the howling depths of winter across some of the harshest terrain on earth, and one that ended with a shoot-out on the Eagle River, February 17, 1932. The man called Albert Johnson had drifted into the North and taken up a hermit-like existence. But when he began encroaching on native traplines, the Mounties went out to his cabin to talk to him. This triggered a chain of events that would eventually leave one officer dead and two others wounded. Johnson fled, setting off a spectacular chase. He ran behind caribou herds, wore his snowshoes backwards, scaled canyon walls, and kicked down avalanches to cover his tracks.

As details emerged about the manhunt, the story of the Mounties versus the Mad Trapper became a media sensation. Canadians and others around the world clamoured for the next newspaper or radio report from the chase.

Legendary bush pilot and former World War One flying ace Wop May was now called in to help. It would be the first time in Canadian history that police had used aerial tracking in the pursuit of a criminal.

May had earlier flown a mercy flight to the remote trading post of Fort Vermilion, Alberta, with a co-pilot in an open-seat plane through minus-40 weather to deliver serum during a diphtheria epidemic. He now joined the hunt for Albert Johnson, not in an open-seat plane this time, but through freezing winds nonetheless, in conditions he would describe as the most fearsome in his career—and this was a man who had tangled with the Red Baron.

The noose slowly began to tighten. As May circled above, Johnson was cornered on the frozen Eagle River. All told, they put at least nine bullets into him. The Mounties had got their man. Wop May landed on the river, and then walked across and stared into the dead man's eyes. Pale blue. No answers.

"Johnson's lips were curled from his teeth in the most terrible sneer I've ever seen," May recalled. "It was the most awful grimace of hate I'll ever see—the hard-boiled, bitter hate of a man who knows he's trapped at last and has determined to take as many enemies as he can with him down the trail he knows he's going to hit . . . . I was glad he was dead. The world seemed a better place with him out of it."

Johnson was photographed and fingerprinted and buried without a past in a graveyard in Aklavik. Is the death grimace in that photograph one of evil? Or mental illness? Cabin-fever run amok? Is it the photograph of a ruthless cunning killer or a lost soul? Or both?

29

Autopsy photo of "Map Trapper" Albert Johnson
after he was gunned down by the RCMP in 1932.

The Dionne quintuplets, 1934.

Five little Dionnes after their Palmolive bath . . . pink as

Now the lovely Dionne Quintuplets use only PALMOLIVE

the soap made wi

VE pairs of chubby little arms
d legs, splashing and churning
water! Five baby voices lifted
ous laughter!

w the Quins love their bat
gentle Palmolive Soap!

the babies that bath is ju
o the specialists in charge it
important matter. And es
important has been the cho
ap gentle enough for the
n of these famous little g

PALMOLIVE WAS CHOSE

the Quins were born pre
y, their skin is unusually
So delicate that it has al
ways required very special care.

Dr. Dafoe himself explains: "At the
time of the birth of the Quintuplets,
time afterward, they

ever touch y

And you too, Lovely Lady . .
you who want to keep your com-
plexion soft, smooth, alluring
through the years! Why not give
your skin the matchless beauty care
that only Palmolive's secret blend
Palm Oils

Canada's Miracle Babies

Dionne quints captivated country, but tragedy loomed

CHRIS WEBB

Why is it that multiple births fascinate us? The stories are inevitably ones of hardship, state intervention, and public scrutiny. From the Dionne quintuplets of 1934 to the Californian octuplets of 2009, fingers are pointed and heads shaken at couples struggling to cope with tons of toddlers.

In the dirty thirties, Ontario Premier Mitchell Hepburn had a rather unique solution for one couple facing many extra mouths to feed: hand them over. It turned out to be a bizarre and tragic family story that became hugely popular with Canadians but ruined the lives of five little girls.

Born to a poor Ontario couple in 1934, Annette, Cécile, Émilie, Marie, and Yvonne were the world's first surviving quintuplets. They were made wards of the state at the age of four months and were kept by the state for the next nine years.

This photograph of Hepburn with his arms outstretched over the quints, as they were called, is a vivid representation of the state's authority over the children. But this is more than a tale of welfare service gone awry. The Ontario government soon realized it could capitalize upon the quints' immense popularity.

The sisters were taken from their parents and moved to the Dafoe Hospital and nursery—right across the street from where they were born in Corbeil, Ontario. But it was no ordinary hospital. For a fee, tourists could watch the sisters play through one-way screens. The quints were taken out for thirty minutes two or three times a day to be paraded before an invisible public. They called it Quintland, and the sisters had no choice but to call it home.

They lived like this from 1934 until 1943, in what Cécile Dionne would later describe as a human zoo. Over 3 million people watched the sisters frolic around in idyllic childhood bliss, far from the hunger, poverty, and suffering of war and economic depression. Their popularity was such that they soon surpassed Niagara Falls as Canada's biggest tourist attraction.

Depression-weary Canadians flocked to the struggling Ontario community to see the quints live the happy lifestyle they wished for their own children. In the depths of misery, theirs was a bright story. Unfortunately, they also became a commodity, as the sales of countless quint "fertility stones" and quint-themed Quaker Oats boxes can attest. It is alleged that the government and nearby businesses made half a billion dollars off tourists, of which the Dionne family saw little.

After an unsuccessful family reunion in November 1943, the sisters moved to Montreal. Annette, Cécile, and Marie took husbands but the marriages failed. Émilie, who had epilepsy, entered a convent and died in 1954. Yvonne eventually worked on behalf of Canadian orphans. The four surviving sisters told their often-bitter tale in the 1965 book *We Were Five*.

In March 1998, the three surviving quints received $4 million in compensation and an apology from the Ontario government.

On-to-Ottawa Trek

Protesters gave voice to impoverished Canadians

PHIL KOCH

It was one of the most tragic events of the Depression years in Canada, and certainly the most violent—a shocking conclusion to what had been among the most hopeful and unifying ventures undertaken during the dirty thirties.

On July 1, 1935—Dominion Day—police moved to break up a peaceful rally, sparking the Regina Riot and ending what had been optimistically dubbed the On-to-Ottawa Trek.

The Great Depression was especially hard on the young, many of whom wandered the country in search of work. Beginning in 1931, relief camps were set up in remote locations across Canada, ostensibly to provide work for the unemployed, but effectively preventing large numbers of young men from congregating in cities and making trouble for the authorities. After the Department of National Defence took over the camps in 1933, workers—who had seen their pay reduced from two dollars a day to twenty cents, plus extremely basic food and accommodations—began to call them "slave camps."

In April 1935, 1,500 men from B.C. relief camps went on strike, gathering in Vancouver to demand improved conditions and benefits. Yet, even after thousands attended rallies in support of the strikers, Prime Minister R.B. Bennett's Conservative government turned a blind eye.

Frustrated by the lack of progress, strike leaders decided early in June to take their protest directly to Ottawa. About 1,000 strikers boarded freight trains and began the On-to-Ottawa Trek. Moving east, the protest gained momentum—and new recruits—at stops in B.C., Alberta, and Saskatchewan. This photo was likely taken at Kamloops, B.C. The trekkers are standing, ready for the train to resume its journey, as a few men hurriedly climb aboard. After years of fruitless toil, they had seized the chance to take action.

By the time they reached Regina on June 14, the trekkers numbered 2,000. Alarmed, Bennett ordered the trains to refuse to carry them any further east. On July 1, the trekkers—still stuck in Regina—gathered for an evening meeting in the city's Market Square to try to find a way out of the impasse.

Bennett, meanwhile, had decided that the trek's leaders must be arrested. When RCMP and city police suddenly charged into the crowd, they set in motion a night of pitched battles with trekkers and Regina citizens. The bloody scuffles left one police detective dead, one protester with a fatal head injury, dozens on both sides injured, 130 men in custody, and the city's downtown heavily damaged.

Most protesters made their way home or back to work camps, but they had gained the sympathies of ordinary Canadians, perhaps even sowing the seeds for a new social welfare system. The Bennett government was voted out that October, and the new Liberal government closed the camps the following year.

Strikers from B.C. relief camps board boxcars
in Kamloops during the On-to-Ottawa Trek, 1935.

Pauline Robertson strains to hear the voice of her husband, David, while he and two other workers remain trapped in the Moose River mine in 1936.

Breaking News

Dramatic radio reports transformed journalism

NELLE OOSTEROM

The woman in the wool coat holds the headphones close against her ears, straining to hear the voice of her husband trapped in a gold mine forty-three metres below. It is April 22, 1936, at Moose River, Nova Scotia. Two survivors have been trapped underground for ten days.

Pauline Robertson is not alone with her anxiety. Millions of people across Canada, the United States, and Europe also have a stake in this drama. They are tuned in to a relatively new medium—radio—and are hearing what is the first-ever live broadcast coverage of a disaster anywhere in the world. And so it was that the Moose River mine disaster became a landmark moment in the history of broadcasting.

It all started on April 12, 1936, when the mine's co-owners, David Robertson and Herman Magill, along with mine employee Alfred Scadding, were trapped in a cave-in. After more than six days, most people had given them up for dead. But then faint tapping sounds were heard. The trapped men were alive! But how to communicate with them? The Maritime Telephone and Telegraph Company came up with the idea to drop a telephone line through the drill hole. While some technicians feverishly invented a microphone small enough to slide inside a one-inch pipe, others extended telephone lines to the mine site.

Radio man J. Frank Willis was late on the scene; radio was considered almost exclusively an entertainment medium back then and his bosses didn't want him to go. But he was quick to size up the potential to use the telephone to bring live coverage to his listeners.

Willis managed to get everyone on a twenty-nine-kilometre party line to agree to keep the phone circuit free. Using a borrowed car as a studio, on April 20 Willis began broadcasting two-minute bulletins at half-hour intervals. A performer by trade, and not a trained journalist, he delivered bulletins that were filled with dramatic flourish. The heartbreak could be heard in Willis's voice when he reported that Magill had succumbed to pneumonia. Then came the terrible news that water was rising up through the rock, threatening to drown the survivors. Listeners hung on to every word of Willis's live reports, which were transmitted to the Canadian Radio Broadcasting Commission (later called the Canadian Broadcasting Corporation) in Ottawa, and from there, to radio stations internationally.

Millions stayed up late to hear Willis announce the end of the ordeal. Robertson and Scadding emerged from the mine shortly after midnight on April 23. "They have been saved," announced Willis, his voice cracking. "They are out of the mine. That is all. This is the Canadian Radio Commission!"

Suddenly, the power of radio to convey breaking news was clear. For the newspapermen who had watched with envy as Willis filed his live reports, it was the beginning of the end of an era. Newspapers would begin a slow decline as they fought ever-increasing competition from radio, television, and now, the Internet.

Remembering Vimy

In the muddy, bloody trenches, a nation was born

RUDYARD GRIFFITHS

When you stand for the first time at Vimy Ridge, it's hard not to think back to that cold April morning in 1917 when 30,000 Canadian soldiers waited in silence along a six-kilometre section of the Allied front.

They looked across a no man's land churned by heavy rains and artillery barrages toward their objective: a hump of land that loomed, as it does now, some 150 metres up out of the surrounding plain. Barnacled with machine gun emplacements, impregnable bunkers, and rows of heavily defended trenches, Vimy Ridge was a truly awesome killing machine that had claimed the lives of upwards of 190,000 French and British soldiers in previous assaults.

On April 9—Easter Monday—a heavy snow began to fall. Huddled in their great coats, the 20,000 front-line Canadian troops waited for the battle to begin. They were volunteers from across Canada, proud of their reputation as a fighting force that inspired fear in the Germans.

Just before 5:30 a.m. the Canadians fixed bayonets. As artillery guns thundered, the soldiers scrambled into no man's land and joined the battle. Advancing behind a creeping artillery barrage, the Canadians found the enemy's barbed wire smashed and forward trenches filled with dazed and surrendering German troops. However, the defences remained near the high point of the ridge—Hill 145.

As the 3rd and 4th divisions moved forward, they were ripped apart by machine guns. The task of taking Hill 145 fell to the Nova Scotia Highlanders. Without artillery support, the Highlanders charged the German guns. Within an hour the position was captured—but it came at a horrific price: roughly 7,000 Canadians wounded and 3,500 dead. Entire battalions were decimated. Towns and cities across Canada shared in this communal loss.

Tragically, the battle at Vimy, like so much of the Great War, proved futile. The British troops fighting with the Canadians at Vimy Ridge had failed to take their objectives; within a week the offensive was over. The next two years would see another 30,000 Canadians killed in the brutal trench warfare. Yet, we rightly remember Vimy as a great national victory. For a country stepping out from behind the apron skirt of the Empire, Vimy represented all that was good in our emerging "Canadian" character.

Canada's frontier ethic of innovation and rugged individualism, coupled with powerful notions of duty and service, fused French, English, immigrants, and aboriginals into a ferocious fighting force. Equally important to Canadians at the time was the recognition by our allies of the great victory we had achieved. With the capture of Vimy Ridge, Canada's consciousness of itself as a nation with a global role and corresponding set of responsibilities was born.

In the final analysis, we need to remember Vimy, and not simply to honour the Canadians who wrestled from the mud of the battlefields of Europe the beginnings our own Canadian identity. Vimy is an enduring reminder that the real test of Canada's greatness lies beyond our shores, when we put our prosperity and privilege into the service of the ideals that we hold dear.

The Vimy Ridge monument, dedicated to Canada's fallen sons, at its unveiling in France, July 26, 1936.

King George VI and Queen Elizabeth, accompanied by Prime Minister Mackenzie King, in Banff, Alberta, May 27, 1939, during the royal cross-country tour.

ck & Son
Finlay

H M KING GEORGE VI   H M QUEEN ELIZABETH

The Ties That Bind

Royal visit a prelude to war

TIM COOK

Rapturous Canadians flocked to see the royal tour of 1939. While there had been British royal tours since the Prince of Wales's trip in 1860, this was the first visit to Canada by a reigning monarch. During the forty-four-day cross-country railway tour in the spring of 1939, King George VI and Queen Elizabeth were greeted by swooning crowds, patriotic songs, heartfelt speeches, and gaudy souvenirs.

Prime Minister William Lyon Mackenzie King soaked up the adoration, recounting the reception in Montreal on May 18, 1939, to his constant companion, his diary: "Along the entire route, people were massed, cheering, cheering and cheering."

Throughout the tour, the ever-present photographers sought to capture the King and Queen for posterity. The camera seemed to bring out the best in the photogenic royals, and their Canadian subjects were very much amused to find that the monarchs seemed human, almost like mid-twentieth-century celebrities.

While this photograph captures the royals at Banff, the royal tour was not simply a benevolent visit. War was coming. Would Canada support the Empire in its time of need, or had the slaughter of the Great War, with its more than 66,000 dead, left the Dominion forever wary of international commitment? Had Canada's full independence over its foreign policy, as revealed in the 1931 Statute of Westminster, finally cut the umbilical cord to Britain? Perhaps the withering effects of the Depression, or the growing American influence on all aspects of Canadian society, had singularly, or collectively, shattered the bonds of Empire? The royal tour was meant to reinforce Canada's ties with the Empire, and to roll back history to a time when blood and belonging ruled the Dominion.

The royal tour took Canada by storm. A few months later, in September 1939, Hitler unleashed his blitzkrieg, dragging the British Empire into war. Canada met its obligations grudgingly—more aware of what another war with Germany would cost, but unwilling to let its monarchs go it alone.

In this photograph of the smiling royals, one is struck by their glamour; the image captures a Hollywoodish quality in their sparkling eyes and cheerful, yet still regal, demeanour. But beneath the smiles is the harder glint of *realpolitik*, with the monarchy as a symbol of imperial unity, the bonds of Empire, and perhaps the subtle chains, too.

Wait for Me, Daddy

Outstretched hands symbolize pain of separation

PHIL KOCH

Like thousands of others across the country, troops of the British Columbia Regiment (Duke of Connaught's Own Rifles) had long been preparing for war when they paraded through New Westminster, B.C., on October 1, 1940. This type of procession was common during the Second World War, but one fleeting moment captured on film by an alert photographer etched the scene in the minds of Canadians and of others around the globe.

Claude Detloff, working for the *Vancouver Daily Province*, was watching the line of troops while keeping an eye on one persistent little boy who was struggling to escape his mother's grip. Then, in an instant, the boy saw his father pass and broke free, reaching out as his father turned back and his mother chased after him. Detloff had only one chance to snap his camera's shutter, and until he developed the film later that day he didn't know what he had. It turned out he had taken a photograph that would represent the sacrifices made by all Canadians during the war.

The next day, the picture of Warren "Whitey" Bernard, then five years old, his father, Private Jack Bernard, and his mother, Bernice, appeared on the front page of the *Province*. It was chosen by *Life* magazine as its photo of the week, then as the North American press photo of the year, and eventually as one of *Life*'s ten best images of the 1940s. The image known as "Wait for me, Daddy" appeared in *Maclean's*, *Time*, the *Encyclopedia Britannica Yearbook*, and countless newspapers.

Young Warren was enlisted in the campaign to support the war effort, appearing alongside Detloff's evocative photograph at the end of variety shows intended to boost the morale of wartime workers and to encourage the purchase of Victory Bonds.

It is difficult now to imagine the scale of the loss experienced during the Second World War. It had an astounding impact on the towns, cities, farms, and businesses that lent it a generation of young men. Families were torn apart for years, if not forever, at a time when keeping in touch meant waiting for letters or notes that would take weeks to arrive from overseas.

All of this is captured in Detloff's photo. The line of departing soldiers walking three abreast stretches up the hill and beyond the horizon, each man carrying a rifle. A few dozen young women walk or stand near the parade, no doubt wondering—like the woman directly behind Warren's mother—what their futures hold. And one boy is forever suspended between the home front and faraway battles.

After seeing action in France and participating in the liberation of Holland, Jack Bernard was among those who made it home safely, and Detloff was at Vancouver's CNR station in late 1944 to capture a reunion hug between father and son.

Thousands of Canadians were not so fortunate to see their loved ones return from war, and this family, like many others, was not to live happily together. Jack and Bernice had grown apart during the years of separation and divorced soon after his homecoming.

"Wait for me, Daddy"—five-year-old Warren runs
to grab the hand of his father, Private Jack Bernard, 1940.

Veronica Foster, popularly known as "Ronnie, the Bren Gun Girl," in Toronto, March 1941.

Our "Rosie the Riveter"

Popular pin-up encouraged women to join war effort

J.L. GRANATSTEIN

Canada was no industrial powerhouse when the nation went to war in September 1939. After a decade of economic depression, the country's gross domestic product was only $5.6 billion and unemployment remained high.

By the end of the Second World War, however, the GDP had more than doubled, unemployment had disappeared, and Canada had turned itself into the fourth-largest producer of military goods among the Allies. For a nation of only 12 million people, this was extraordinary.

As men left the factories to fight on the front lines, women were recruited to take their place and began turning out the ships, aircraft, artillery shells, and machine guns that would help turn the tide against the Nazis. The women came in the tens of thousands, many leaving farms and villages for high-paying work in the munitions factories. By 1943, there were 261,000 women working in wartime industry—more than a quarter of Canada's million-strong work force.

Today, when we think about women's contributions to the war effort, we likely picture "Rosie the Riveter"—the iconic American woman war worker. Rosie's Canadian equivalent was the "Bren Gun Girl," shown here in a photograph taken in March 1941 at the John Inglis Co. Ltd. plant in Toronto. The Bren Gun Girl was Veronica "Ronnie" Foster, who operated a lathe and turned out Bren light machine guns for the army. Foster was featured in a series of National Film Board propaganda photos aimed at encouraging women to join the workforce. This photo—which shows the beautiful Ronnie Foster with her hair in a bandana and her face wreathed in smoke as she takes a break on the production line—became famous during the war.

The weapons Foster and her fellow workers produced were essential. Every infantry platoon of thirty men had three Brens, and Inglis turned out thousands. The Bren was relatively inexpensive, simple to build, and easy to fire, and it worked in the mud and the cold. Without the Bren Gun Girl and those like her, the Canadian war industry could not have done the job.

And what a job; in one typical week in 1943, Canada's war industry produced six vessels, 80 aircraft, 4,000 trucks and jeeps, 450 armoured fighting vehicles, 940 artillery pieces, 13,000 weapons, 525,000 artillery shells, 25 million cartridges, ten tonnes of explosives, and $4 million worth of instruments and communications equipment. None of this could have been accomplished without a quarter-million Ronnie Fosters.

At war's end, most of the military work disappeared. The John Inglis Co. Ltd. resumed producing household appliances, and returning veterans reclaimed their jobs. Most of the Bren Gun Girls left the shop floor, married, and became homemakers. Most were happy to get off the production lines, but some resented that the days of high pay had ended.

The Roaring Lion

Iconic image was a wartime beacon of hope

DON NEWMAN

It was just weeks after the attack on Pearl Harbor, and days after the fall of Hong Kong.

On December 30, 1941, Winston Churchill, the British prime minister, was in Ottawa to address a special joint session of the Canadian Parliament. The war in Europe had been raging for the past two years, and Canadian troops had been in England for almost all of that time. Churchill was in Canada to say thank you—and to try to maintain popular support for the war— with a speech broadcast across the country from the floor of the House of Commons.

The speech would produce many stirring moments, including Churchill's famously defiant line—"Some neck. Some chicken!"—used to rebuke the French generals who had predicted Hitler would quickly wring England's neck after the fall of France. However, it would be a photograph taken during Churchill's Canadian visit that would immortalize both the British leader and the man who shot the image.

The story of how Yousuf Karsh transformed a British bulldog into a "Roaring Lion" is itself legendary. At the conclusion of Churchill's speech to Parliament, Canadian Prime Minister William Lyon Mackenzie King escorted his British counterpart past the Speaker's chair and out the back door of the House of Commons, into what is known as the Speaker's corridor. King wanted a photograph to commemorate Churchill's visit and had arranged to borrow the Speaker's office for the photo shoot. King had also commissioned a rising Ottawa photographer to snap the photo—Karsh, who, seventeen years before, had emigrated from Turkey to Canada at the age of sixteen.

All King had neglected to do was tell Churchill. In the corridor, Churchill had lit one of his signature cigars. He was not expecting—and at first resisted—having his photograph taken. But King managed to steer him into the Speaker's wood-panelled office and introduced him to Karsh.

As Karsh framed the shot, Churchill was scowling, and still smoking his cigar. Karsh offered him an ashtray, but Churchill refused. Karsh checked his focus and picked up his shutter release. Then, he suddenly reached out and snatched the cigar out of Churchill's mouth. The British prime minister's scowl immediately deepened—and with the click of Karsh's camera, history was made.

Karsh's photo, later christened "The Roaring Lion," gave heart to millions of people around the world looking for a spark of hope amid the darkness of the Second World War. Since then, the image has been reproduced countless times.

Three copies of the famous photo are on display in Ottawa: at the Chateau Laurier, where Karsh kept a studio and lived for many years; at the historic Rideau Club, of which Karsh was a member; and on Parliament Hill, in the office of the Speaker of the House of Commons—hanging on the very panel which appeared behind the British prime minister when "The Roaring Lion" was immortalized in 1941.

37

A scowling Prime Minister Winston Churchill is captured
in this photograph taken by Yousuf Karsh in December 1941

The aftermath of the disastrous raid on Dieppe, August 19, 1942.

38

Disaster at Dieppe

Hopeless battle tested limits of bravery

JOEL RALPH

Bravery can push men to try anything—including the impossible—and even, sometimes, to accomplish it. But August 19, 1942, is a date when the limits of bravery were underscored for Canadian and Allied forces fighting in the Second World War.

Nearly three years into the conflict, the Second Canadian Infantry Division, supported by British and American commandos, crossed the English Channel and landed in full force to test the German defences at the small French seaside town of Dieppe. The lightning-quick attack was to commence just before daybreak. Troops were tasked with securing the town, and then moving inland to capture a nearby airfield and radar station before withdrawing to the sea.

The raid was a disaster. From the water's edge and up the beach Canadian infantry and tanks, along with Royal Navy landing craft, were decimated. The infantry was pinned down by withering fire and unable to advance across an open esplanade to the oceanfront buildings. Without infantry support to clear the roadblocks, the handful of brand new Churchill tanks that made it off the beach were unable to enter the town. Flanking attacks designed to free up the massive heights that guarded each side of the town also foundered without support from armoured units still stuck on the main beach.

As this photo—shot by victorious German troops—shows, the Canadians had nowhere to go, and the beach became a killing field. The smooth stones lining the bodies of the dead Canadian soldiers exploded in all directions as mortars and shells fell, causing numerous casualties. Even worse, the tanks' carefully constructed treads spun wearily, unable to gain any traction, until stones finally slipped between the belts and broke them down completely at the water's edge.

In a last-ditch effort, Royal Navy crews beached their landing craft to retrieve the remaining survivors. Some of the worst casualties were suffered as men made one last run for freedom. A few ships escaped, though most were either swamped with men or destroyed by German defences, bolstered with each passing minute. Harassed throughout the battle by unseen enemies hiding in the cliffs, by carefully protected German artillery, and by streaking Nazi fighters and bombers, the Canadians had no chance for success on that forsaken beach.

Over 900 Canadians died in the few hours of battle that day. Nearly 2,000 more were captured, many of them wounded. They would wait out the rest of the war in German prisoner of war camps.

Each year, thousands of Canadians make their own pilgrimage to Dieppe. They stand at the water's edge, staring up at the cliff faces guarding the beach and the more than 200 metres of open ground before the town. The weight of impossibility rests heavily on their shoulders, knowing the destruction that took place. At the water's edge they ponder the limits of bravery and remember the sacrifice we asked of our soldiers that day.

For King and Country

Savvy PM orchestrated picture-perfect meeting

DESMOND MORTON

Imagine it: the two iconic Western leaders of the Second World War, Franklin Delano Roosevelt and Winston Spencer Churchill, come to Quebec City in August, 1943. Who is the plump, dark-suited man sitting beside them? Canada's William Lyon Mackenzie King, that's who.

The background is the outer wall of Quebec's Citadel. Below it, the St. Lawrence River broadens on its surge to the sea. In a conference code-named "Quadrant," Roosevelt and Churchill met to plan a victorious strategy for their war against Hitler's Germany, Mussolini's Italy, and Hideki Tojo's Japan. Out of the first Quebec Conference came decisions to invade Europe in 1944, and to intensify the Pacific War so that, if need be, Japan's defeat would follow Germany's by no more than a year. And in an agreement so secret most historians ignore it, the United States also agreed to share the secrets of its atomic bomb with Great Britain.

The decisions made at this conference would eventually bring victory at a cost of about 30,000 more Canadian lives.

At the time, Canadians—entering the fourth year of the war—found the presence of their prime minister among the great leaders of the conflict profoundly satisfying. If Canada had emerged from the First World War with the identity of a near-sovereign nation, the Quebec conference seemed to signal that Canadians now helped make Allied decisions about how the war would be waged.

By no coincidence, that was exactly what their crafty prime minister wanted them to think.

Offering the historic Quebec Citadel as a site for the British and American leaders was seen as an opportunity for Canadians to play a leadership role in the war. Sir Robert Borden, King's predecessor as a wartime prime minister, had undoubtedly played such a role in 1917 and 1918.

King, though, was more cautious. His real policy was to avoid the Canadian mistakes of the earlier Great War. One of them, he believed, was Borden's assertiveness. Perhaps Canada's toll of more than 60,000 dead might have been lower, and the Conscription Crisis of 1917 averted, if Borden had been less eager to show leadership.

King wanted a Canadian voice in Allied policy only when Canadian interests were directly involved. However, King also worried that the rival Conservatives might gain an advantage by portraying him as a timid leader compared to Churchill and Roosevelt.

In the end, it was agreed that Canada would not be part of the official Quadrant sessions—and this was just fine with King. He recognized that most Canadians would be entirely satisfied to see him playing host to the U.S. president and British prime minister.

This photograph was precisely what King wanted from this historic occasion. Canada's role at the Quebec Conference, as official historian Charles Stacey recalled, was to provide the whiskey and the soda, plus what political and media hacks call "photo ops." Sometimes we see King talking earnestly to Roosevelt; in others he is addressing a faintly amused Churchill. Was he trying to change the course of human history? No—he was thinking about postwar elections.

TOP SECRET

William Lyon Mackenzie King, Franklin D. Roosevelt, and Winston Churchill
smile for the cameras at the first Quebec Conference, August 1943.

Canadian soldiers landing at Nan White beach on D-Day, June 6, 1944.

On the Beach

D-Day photo showed Canada taking fight to the Nazis

J.L. GRANATSTEIN

The reserve brigade had a relatively leisurely landing on Juno Beach, the men disembarking from their landing craft and wading ashore. Some—they can be seen at the water's edge in the photograph—even carried the bicycles that some too-clever staff officers hoped would speed the troops on their way inland. On the beach, all was organized chaos with heavy armoured equipment and men moving every which way, but with most heading inland ready to fight the Germans.

A few hours earlier on D-Day, June 6, 1944, the scene had been very different. The Americans, British, and Canadians had come ashore in Normandy, their landing craft weaving around the obstacles placed in the water. Above, bombers and fighters flew, their aim to drench the beach defences with fire. Offshore, the big guns of great battleships fired at blockhouses and gun positions.

But it was up to the infantrymen to brave the Germans' machine guns and clean out their bunkers. Company Sergeant-Major Charlie Martin's company of the Queen's Own Rifles were in the first wave, and every man had been well trained for what he was to do. As Martin's landing craft came closer to the shore, he thought that he had never been so alone in his life. "Ten boats stretched out over 1,500 yards is not really a whole lot of assault force," he recalled, and the Sherman tanks supporting the Queen's Own were late. Worse, the soldiers could see the enemy's pillboxes and obstacles manned and untouched by bombs or shellfire. And once the boats grounded in full daylight, machine gun and mortar fire began to fall heavily on the beach.

Success depended on junior leaders, on the courage of the soldiers, and the initiative of every man. D-Day succeeded, but it was a closer run than the historians tell us. Men like Martin made the difference. "Move! Fast! Don't stop for anything! Go! Go! Go!" he had shouted at his mates. And they did.

The riflemen of the Queen's Own, much like those of the Royal Winnipeg Rifles, the North Shore Regiment, and the Regina Rifles, made all the difference between victory and defeat. One German gun wiped out most of a platoon of riflemen before the Canadians could knock it out. Another half company of Canadian troops fell to machine gun fire from a large concrete bunker.

Many soldiers never even made it onto the beach. Jim Wilkins, a Queen's Own rifleman, recalled being hit by bullets three times just moments after jumping out of a landing craft: "By this time I was flat on my face in the water. . . . The man beside me is dead. . . ."

But others survived, their training taking over. Men crawled into position to toss grenades into enemy bunkers, and engineers soon bulldozed exits through the sandbanks so the tanks could move inland. Regrouping, their leaders taking hold, the Canadians moved forward. And, as this photo proved, they were in France to stay.

Sweet Liberty

Canadians' sacrifices won Dutch salvation

PETER MANSBRIDGE

If they had ever wondered what they were fighting for, this was their answer. This is why Canadian soldiers had fought in Italy, landed on D-Day on the beaches of Normandy, battled across France and Belgium. And this is why they had endured nine grueling months of pain and sacrifice to push the Nazis out of Holland.

They had done it to liberate an oppressed people.

The Dutch had suffered under German occupation for five years. The last winter was the worst, the freezing cold "Hunger Winter" of 1945. The Germans had stopped all transportation of food from outside Holland. Then, as they retreated under fire, they destroyed vital transportation routes within the country and flooded farmland. The Dutch were reduced to eating tulip bulbs and sugar beets to stay alive.

The Jews of Holland had been hunted to near extinction. There were 140,000 when the war started; just 30,000 remained alive on liberation day.

So what you see on the faces of these Dutch men and women, these survivors, is pure joy. And you see, in their outstretched arms, their desperate need to express gratitude to the men who have saved them. The only Canadian in the picture is the most calm. A half smile on his face, his hat raised in salute, he seems a little surprised at the reception.

There is, of course, no room for sentiment in planning war strategy, but it was fitting that Canadian troops liberated the Netherlands. The Dutch royal family had escaped to Canada for safety and lived in Ottawa during the war. A royal baby, Princess Margriet, was born there.

Surveys regularly show that most Canadians are abysmally ignorant of our Second World War history. The Dutch, on the other hand, have never forgotten what Canada did for them in the conflict. Even those who were born after the war have been taught that they owe a debt to Canadians. People who live in Holland today have been faithful to their ancestors in this photo. They have never stopped expressing their deep and eternal gratitude to the liberators. That is most poignantly reflected at the Canadian war cemeteries in Holland. Each has perfectly tended grounds, and at many of the 7,000 graves you will often see flowers, placed there by Dutch schoolchildren.

A photo like this serves as a vital window to the past. Though it would be impossible to ever recapture the raw emotion of this scene, it is possible from time to time to get a sense of how deep the feelings are for Canadians in Holland.

Canadian veterans are invited back every year on Liberation Day. On major anniversaries, the welcome is especially exuberant. To mark the fiftieth and sixtieth anniversaries (May 1995 and May 2005), there were high-spirited parades in the town of Apeldoorn. The liberators, some now in their eighties and nineties, rode through the streets as a grateful population saluted them with cheers, flowers, hugs, and kisses. One woman brought her baby to the parade route. When asked why, she said, "I wanted him to see what a Canadian is."

Jubilation in Utrecht as Canadian soldiers liberate Holland, May 7, 1945.

41

Oscar Peterson with his father, Daniel, playing piano together, September 1945.

42

Hymns of Freedom

Canadian jazz giant believed music was colour-blind

MARK REID

There have been many photos taken of Oscar Peterson that showcase the mastery this iconic Montrealer had over the ivories.

But none better capture Peterson's joy of playing—and the limitless potential of the future jazz giant—than this early shot, taken in 1945 for the Canadian Pacific Railway's staff magazine.

Eyes upturned, the nineteen-year-old Peterson beams into the camera as his father, Daniel, sits beside him. What the picture doesn't show, though, is the growing anger he felt over the racism he was encountering in his budding career.

A child virtuoso, Peterson got his big break in 1940, when, at age fourteen, he won a CBC talent show. Five years later—by then already a household name in Montreal—the nineteen-year-old Peterson starred on CBC's *Merchant Navy Show* as the "coloured boy" with the "amazing fingers" who was "cutting a blazing path to success." In later years, Peterson admitted he had felt insulted by the announcer's repeated use of the word "boy" during the interview. His father had also encountered bigotry while working as a porter for the CPR; this greatly influenced the younger Peterson, driving him to use his music to bridge the gap between black and white.

Peterson was soon wowing crowds throughout Canada and the United States. In the southern U.S., he was allowed to entertain white people, but not to eat with them. Being black, he was banned from many restaurants; he had to eat in the car while his white band-mates ate inside.

At times, Peterson would get it from both sides. In 1953, he formed the Oscar Peterson trio, along with bassist Ray Brown, who was black, and guitarist Herb Ellis, who was white. Ellis's presence angered some white bigots, while some black fans felt betrayed that Peterson had recruited a white man to play "their" music.

As the turbulent 1960s unfolded, Peterson was inspired by the civil rights movement to write one of the most beautiful and enduring pieces in jazz, the bluesy "Hymn to Freedom." The lyrics, written at Peterson's request by Harriette Hamilton, speak to the power of music to break down racial barriers: "When every man joins in our song and together singing harmony, / That's when we'll be free."

Peterson would go on to thrill audiences for another thirty years. Slowed somewhat by a stroke in 1993, he continued to play, although with a diminished technique. When he passed away in December 2007, the legends of jazz gathered in Toronto to send him off with a musical tribute.

In his autobiography, Peterson said he feared for jazz's place in the musical lexicon. He worried that jazz—with its roots in the black experience—would always be fated to sit at the back of the musical bus.

He needn't have worried. Perhaps the greatest testament to Peterson's legacy came in early 2009, when his "Hymn to Freedom" was performed during the inauguration of Barack Obama, America's first black president.

Shameful "Repatriation"

Japanese Canadians railroaded into moving to Japan

J.L. GRANATSTEIN

Arms crossed, a woman in this photo waits pensively for a train that will take her and the rest of these Japanese Canadians to the coast. From there, they would be shipped back to their "homeland"—a beaten and war-battered Japan that most of them had never even visited. It's an image, and an event, that today evokes feelings of shame. But in postwar Canada, most Canadians supported the "repatriation" of Japanese Canadians.

Racism was the norm in Canada in the years leading up to the Second World War. In British Columbia, those of Asian origin were singled out for special abuse. As Japan became a military and naval power in the Pacific, Japanese Canadians—especially the 23,000 living in coastal B.C.—took a special place in the racist litany.

Most Japanese Canadians had been born in Canada and were British subjects, but Japan considered them Japanese citizens. The consulate in Vancouver was active in the community, and, as we know now, busy recruiting spies to collect military information. Many Japanese Canadians had supported Japan in its war with China prior to the 1941 attack on Pearl Harbor.

Ottawa had been concerned about Japanese Canadians for some time. Immediately after war in the Pacific began, it seized their fishing boats and radios, and soon thereafter, the RCMP rounded up Japanese Canadian men of military age and sent them to work camps in the B.C. interior. In late 1942, the federal government evacuated the remaining old men, women, and children to rough townsites deep inland. They then sold off their property at fire-sale prices—a move met with widespread approval across Canada, especially from those who benefited. The federal government also interned 758 men who were active supporters of Imperial Japan or who protested too vigorously against the evacuation.

By 1944, fear of Japanese attack on the Pacific coast had disappeared, but the opposition to Japanese Canadians remained. Evacuees in the B.C. camps were told they could leave as long as they moved east, and many took jobs in Alberta sugar beet fields or in factories. The government also coldly decided to return some Japanese Canadians to a Japan most had never seen. The original intention was to deport all of them, but this draconian policy raised protests from civil libertarians, so the federal government decided on a "voluntary" program. Under heavy pressure, 10,397 decided to return to Japan. Many spoke no Japanese, and by 1946, thousands changed their minds and opted to remain in Canada.

In the end, 3,964 people—including the men, women, and children shown in this photograph, taken at Slocan, B.C.—returned to Japan. The remaining 20,000 spread out across Canada, overcame the past, and became extraordinarily productive Canadians.

The wartime treatment of Japanese Canadians was far from Canada's finest hour. Not until 1988 did Canada apologize to its Japanese Canadians for the sins of wartime.

Japanese Canadians, who were allowed to take only whatever possessions they could carry, await deportation to Japan, Slocan City, B.C., 1946.

43

44

A column of smoke and flame erupts from Imperial Oil's Leduc #1, February 13, 1947.

Alberta's Black Gold

Gusher sparked oil boom in the West

CHRISTOPHER MOORE

Vern Hunter, the toolpush, had recognized the signs days earlier, and the word went out. There was oil down there, a kilometre and a half below the Turta family farm outside Leduc, Alberta. Now they only had to turn the valve.

Almost 500 people gathered; it was a cold, sunny Thursday afternoon. The lieutenant governor came. A cabinet minister helped turn the valve, and an Edmonton radio station recorded the rumble of the rising oil. There were Imperial Oil executives and scouts for rival companies. Quite a few of the local farmers came, Polish and Ukrainian Canadians from the families that had opened up the area fifty years earlier. They all hoped to witness history in the making. And they did.

By then, Southern Alberta had been producing natural gas for decades. In the 1930s, oil finds at Turner Valley drew the big oil companies to Alberta and turned the nearby cow town of Calgary into the West's oil capital. But by the end of the Second World War, production was in decline. Were there new fields to find? Executives at Imperial Oil contemplated a grim record of unsuccessful exploration and wondered if they should look in South America. Vern Hunter, who would direct the drilling at Leduc, had learned his trade at Turner Valley, but since then his track record had earned him a nickname: "Dry Hole" Hunter.

The science of oil exploration was still in its infancy in the 1940s, but it was cutting-edge petroleum geology that sent the drill rigs north to the country around Edmonton, where a 400-million-year-old tropical reef from the Devonian era lay buried deep beneath the prairie. Could there be oil in Devonian rock? Seismic surveyors began setting off small explosions underground, and charted the echoes to reveal the rock formations. Their charts turned up an "anomaly" deep below Leduc. Vern Hunter's crew drilled Leduc #1 into the heart of it.

They drilled through the winter, grousing about indifferent food, bad weather, snow and mud, coping with cold so deep they hardly dared shut off the trucks overnight. But 1,525 metres down, the signs of oil were strong.

On February 13, 1947, they spun the valve that opened the hole. The first burps became a steady roar. An oil geyser erupted from the wellhead. At Hunter's signal, they ignited the natural gas plume. The photographer had the shot of the year: raw power, money to burn.

Before Leduc, Alberta produced barely 6 million barrels of oil a year. The Leduc field proved out at 300 million barrels. A year later, the Redwater field, just north of Edmonton, yielded another 900 million barrels. Alberta had oil production for generations. Leduc #1 changed Alberta and the West forever. High finance. Industry. Population growth. Wealth, national clout, and global influence. They all flowed from Vern Hunter's drill bit.

Life had always been a struggle for the families who farmed around Leduc. "Farming is a lot easier when you have oil," said one of them.

Faces of Hope

Rescue from Nazis came too late for many

IRVING ABELLA

There were not many European Jews who survived the Holocaust. And there were almost no children. More than 1.5 million Jewish children were murdered by the Nazis. The youngsters in this photograph, smiling and full of hope, were among the handful of those who were spared. And almost all of them were orphans, without families, homes, or even countries they could go back to.

Canada would be their new home. Just over 1,000 Jewish orphans were allowed into Canada in the years 1947 to 1949—but not without a fight. For the previous twenty years, Canada had restricted the flow of Jews into the country. These children were part of the first large group of Jews admitted into Canada since the 1920s. Indeed, in the period between 1933, when Hitler came to power in Germany, and 1945, when the Second World War ended—when European Jews were being hunted down and killed—Canada firmly closed her doors to Jewish refugees.

Partly because of the Depression, but mostly because of the anti-Semitism that permeated the country in these years, the Canadian government—with much popular support—decided not to admit more than a sprinkling of Jews. Of all the Western democracies, and of all the immigration countries, Canada had by far the worst record in rescuing Jews: While Canada accepted some 3,000, the United States took 150,000; Argentina 50,000; tiny Palestine 100,000; and beleaguered Great Britain took 90,000.

Even in the midst of the war, when presented with an opportunity of saving several thousand Jewish children from Vichy France, the Canadian government demurred. Officials explained that it was government policy to admit only entire family units—and in any case, it would be embarrassing to Canada if, after the war, these "orphans" then sponsored their parents as immigrants. When the cabinet finally agreed to pass a special order-in-council to accept one thousand children ranging in age from six months to ten years, it was too late. The Nazis had moved first and had shipped these orphans to Auschwitz, where all of them were murdered.

Fortunately for the children in this photo, the order-in-council was never rescinded. Reactivated in 1947 following a determined lobbying campaign by the Canadian Jewish Congress, it was this cabinet document that finally opened Canada's doors to the first contingent of Jewish refugees from the displaced persons' camps in Europe.

Tragically, it proved impossible to find 1,000 "children." The Nazis had been so thorough and merciless in ferreting out Jews that very few under the age of ten survived. Under pressure from the Jewish community, the federal government agreed to accept orphans who were well into their teens, and even beyond. Only in that way could they meet the goal of 1,000.

The children in this photo were among the youngest to arrive. And, like the 1,000 or so others, they were adopted by Jewish families across the country.

Jewish orphans board a bus in Paris en route to new homes in Canada, April 27, 1947.

45

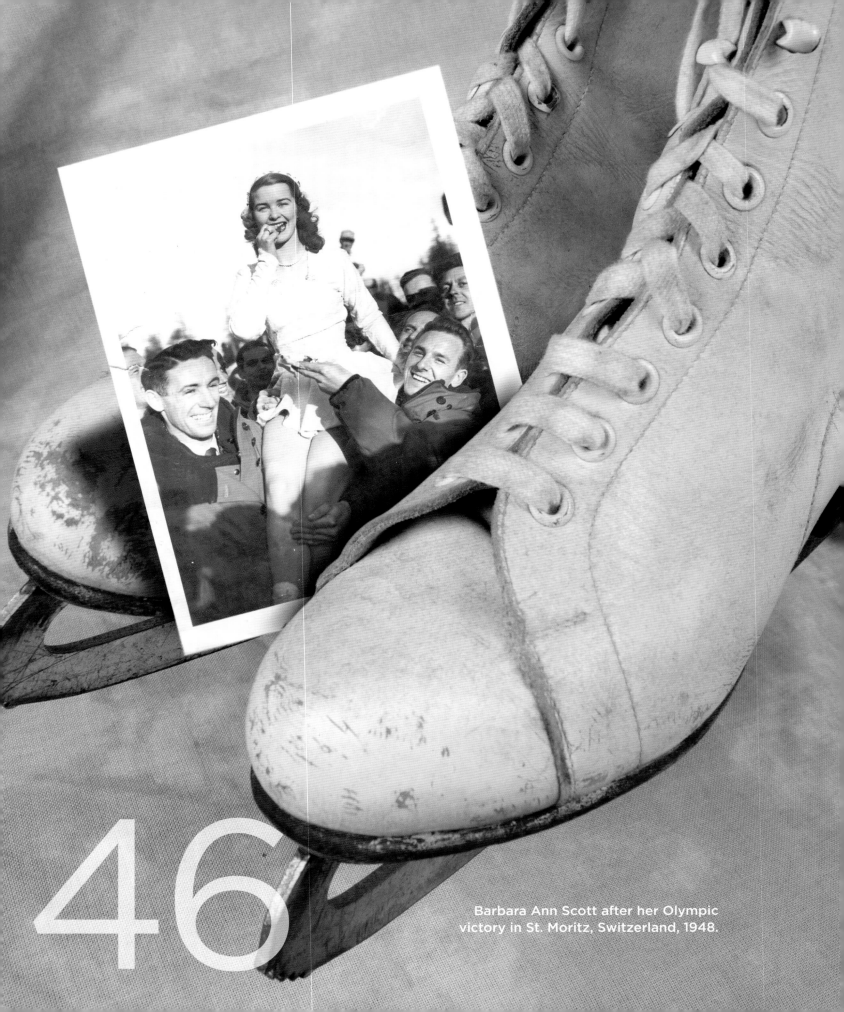

46

Barbara Ann Scott after her Olympic
victory in St. Moritz, Switzerland, 1948.

Sweet Victory

Canadian skater won hearts—and medals

RICHARD W. POUND

No one in Canadian sport history has attracted the level of public adoration lavished on Barbara Ann Scott, the petite winner of the gold medal in figure skating at the 1948 Olympic Winter Games in the Swiss resort of St. Moritz.

She had become Canadian junior ladies champion in 1939, and while her progress was slowed by the Second World War, she was dominant thereafter, winning the senior ladies championship in 1944, 1945, 1946, and 1948; the North American ladies championship in 1945, 1946, 1947, and 1948; and the European and world championships in 1947 and 1948.

In postwar Canada, patriotism and national pride had emerged from the country's remarkable contribution to the Allied victory. Barbara Ann Scott—beautiful, graceful, talented, and a winner—was soon adopted by Canadians as a unifying symbol of that pride.

Her 1948 Olympic victory propelled her onto the world stage in a manner unequalled by any other sporting event. In this photograph, she is carried on the shoulders of her delighted teammates, smiling and nibbling on a piece of—what else for Canada's sweetheart?—sweet Swiss chocolate.

Only a year before, however, there had been no such smile on her face. Scott had been the centre of a major controversy in the spring of 1947 that almost kept her out of the Olympics. It began with the seemingly innocuous presentation of a yellow convertible by the people of Ottawa, a spontaneous gift in recognition of the skater's extraordinary achievements.

The trouble was that the act of accepting the gift compromised her amateur status, a preoccupation with both the International Olympic Committee and the Canadian Olympic Association responsible for enforcing the prevailing dogma of amateurism. Such were her fame and the publicity attracted by the gift that the question of her eligibility immediately became a matter of concern, both at home and in anticipation of complaints from other Olympic committees.

Politicians used the occasion for polemic questioning of Olympic organizations in Canada and the IOC. Ottawa Mayor Stanley Lewis launched an attack on Olympic officials. John Diefenbaker, in opposition at the time, raised a question in the House of Commons, to which Prime Minister Mackenzie King (typically) did not reply (although King did write to the Canadian IOC member, asking him to do what he could to resolve the matter satisfactorily).

The tempest subsided when Scott returned the car. The return was almost as well publicized as the gift, with newspaper reports and headlines declaring "Car Ceremony Brings Tears" and photographs showing the skater kissing the convertible, with the caption "Good-bye Old Pal."

Forty years after this photograph, Scott, still a Canadian darling, was the first torchbearer in the first Olympic Winter Games held in Canada—1988's Calgary Games. By this time, the amateur rules that had bedevilled Barbara Ann Scott had been repealed in favour of a more modern approach to the realities and attendant costs of international sport.

Never Rise Again

A banner day for Newfoundland and Canada

HON. BRIAN V. TOBIN

The old flag did fall, but it did not come down easily.

It would take two referenda in 1948—held on June 3 and on July 22—to determine Newfoundland and Labrador's political future.

The Great Depression and the Second World War that followed set the stage for a fiercely independent-minded people to seriously consider union with Canada. The Dominion of Newfoundland's earlier financial contribution to the First World War, along with the ravages of the dirty thirties, left the government broke and unable to borrow even for its basic needs.

Following an appeal to Britain for help in 1934, representative government was suspended and the British government appointed a Commission of Government to look after Newfoundland's affairs. For the next fifteen years, six appointed commissioners—in the absence of any consideration of the democratic will of the people—would carry on the ordinary work of government. During this period, the commission would largely fail in its efforts to stimulate the economy and improve the quality of life in Newfoundland.

Indeed, it was the advent of the Second World War, and not the work of the commission, that ultimately changed Newfoundland's economic and political fortunes. Its geographical location made it strategically important for the war effort. The arrival of naval and air force personnel, and the construction of military bases by both the Canadian and American forces, all led to sudden prosperity. Newfoundlanders were working shoulder to shoulder with both Canadian and American military personnel, and building confidence in themselves as the war effort progressed. It soon became clear that there would be no going back to an undemocratic Commission of Government once the great battle against tyranny was over.

By 1945, Britain itself was financially exhausted; it could no longer financially support Newfoundland and Labrador. Newfoundlanders, meanwhile, were brimming with optimism. The military bases established during the war seemed permanent and, in fact, installations were being expanded. Centres like St. John's, Gander, Goose Bay, and Stephenville were booming.

The same was not true for the small outport fishing communities. It is no small wonder, then, that the subsequent referendum battle lines shaped up between rural and urban Newfoundland. The pro-Confederation movement found its strength in rural areas, while the anti-Confederation forces—led by St. John's merchant families—launched their campaign from the capital city. Adding to the rural-urban divide was the entry into the campaign of the Roman Catholic Church, which, fearing for the future of denominational schools, came out forcefully against union with Canada. When the final ballots were counted, Newfoundlanders—divided by both religion and geography—had narrowly voted to become Canada's tenth province.

And so the old flag fell. It was a flag that presided over the division of a people. May it never rise again. Today, the Maple Leaf flies proudly everywhere in Newfoundland and Labrador—a unifying symbol of the values shared by all Canadians.

A boy holds up the former flag of Newfoundland following Confederation with Canada, 1949.

47

WE LET THE OLD FLAG FALL.

COME into my PARLOR!

HUDSON BAY

LABRADOR, NFLD.

48

Fireman rescues a child from a burning building, Calgary, 1949.

PRESS CAR

Accredited Reporter on the Staff
extended will b

Unflinching Eye

Tragic photo set the standard for photojournalists

GRAEME ROY

It's a scene of obvious urgency, an instant frozen in time by the harsh light of a photographer's flash. Clutching a small child who appears lifeless, a firefighter rushes from a house with smoke billowing from the windows. Another man is trying to climb out of a window, his head surrounded by smoke.

The photo, shot by *Calgary Herald* photographer Jack DeLorme in 1949 and the first National Newspaper Award winner for spot news, helped to usher in a new era of news photography in Canada, where the photographer was elevated from record-taker of stiffly staged events to storyteller.

For reader and photojournalist alike, it is a heart-breaking image. (The story became all the more tragic when the child died later in hospital.) But it is a not uncommon scene that working photojournalists encounter at times in their careers and, as chilling or gruesome or hard to take as a photo like this is, it is their job to make sure the wider world knows what happened.

The public's reaction to a news story told visually is heavily influenced by how closely it strikes home—both physically and emotionally. The physical proximity of the scene of a photo, for instance, can have a large impact on a reader's reaction. A photo of a tragedy on the other side of the planet, viewed from the safety of a reader's comfortable family room, does not strike with the same force as a photo taken down the street.

Photojournalists are often the first witnesses to history and it's their job to record it—even when faced with a scene that may irrevocably scar them. How can one not be affected when faced by scenes of tragedy or despair?

Photojournalists constantly engage in an ethical debate over whether to air the photos they shoot. For some viewers, these images may be hard to view. But photographers must weigh these concerns against their ultimate goal—searching for and publishing the truth of the news events that shape us and the world in which we live.

It is one thing, for instance, to read that twenty-five people were killed in a car bombing, but quite another to actually view the full terror and chaos of the event through the lens of a photographer.

The role of photojournalists is to document truth as they witness it, regardless of how emotionally devastating it might be. A greater good is ultimately served when even harsh realities are preserved on a camera and brought to light.

Cold War Bag Man

Soviet defector's spy stories stunned the nation

TIM COOK

To see the man with the bag on his head was always a strange sight, but he was well known to most Canadians. The bag man is Igor Gouzenko, an intriguing figure in Canadian history. He was a catalyst for identifying the Cold War between the superpowers of the United States and the Soviet Union, and their respective allies. Few could have anticipated that the origin of the Cold War might be pinpointed to the sleepy Canadian government town of Ottawa.

Just a few weeks after the war with Japan ended with the dropping of the atomic bomb, a low-level cipher clerk in the Soviet Embassy in Ottawa defected with incriminating documents that revealed an intricate spy ring in the Canadian capital. With little planning, the panicking Gouzenko fled his embassy on September 5, 1945, armed only with his pilfered files.

With Soviet agents tracking him, Gouzenko gathered his wife and infant son and looked for asylum with the RCMP. Word of the spy ring almost caused the timid Canadian prime minister, William Lyon Mackenzie King, to hand Gouzenko back to the Soviets—and to his certain death—for fear of what this international incident would spawn.

More courageous heads prevailed. Gouzenko was interrogated, and his information was shared with the United States and Great Britain. It was then used to publicly embarrass the Soviets in February 1946 by arresting the spies. Gouzenko was the first major Soviet defector, and he revealed that within the dying embers of the Second World War a new fire waited to ignite the superpowers.

In 1948, Gouzenko published a bestselling autobiography, *This Was My Choice*. Six years later, he published a novel about Soviet life, called *The Fall of a Titan*. In this 1954 photo, Gouzenko shares a moment with actress Irja Jensen, who played Svetlana in *Operation Manhunt*, a 1954 film about Gouzenko.

In the 1950s, he had begun to wear a bag on his head while in public, supposedly to trick Soviet assassins—although one could hardly think of a better way to attract attention. This he certainly did among the normally staid Ottawa residents.

While Gouzenko eventually faded from the limelight, he was a Cold War celebrity, and his defection allowed Canadians to imagine themselves as significant players in the new Cold War. They were not, although the man with the bag on his head remained an intriguing and exotic character in a country generally bereft of such figures.

49

Igor Gouzenko speaks with actress Irja Jensen—who appeared in *Operation Manhunt*, a 1954 film about Gouzenko—on April 14, 1954.

50

Angry fan attacks NHL President Clarence Campbell during
the Richard Riot in Montreal, March 17, 1955.

The Richard Riot

Star's suspension bodychecked Quebecers

JACQUES LACOURSIÈRE

On March 17, 1955, the city of Montreal was the scene of one of the most significant riots in NHL history.

Fans of the Montreal Canadiens could not accept the fact that their idol, Maurice "Rocket" Richard, was the victim of what they considered to be a great injustice.

The fury began at the Montreal Forum, when angry fans attacked Clarence Campbell, the president of the National Hockey League (Campbell is seen in this photo holding his hat as he recoils from a rioter). The violence then spilled out onto the city streets. A dozen police officers were injured and scores of wounded spectators had to be transported to hospital.

It had all begun in Boston four days earlier, on March 13. The Canadiens were in town to play the Bruins. In the fourteenth minute of the third period, an altercation broke out between the Bruins' Hal Laycoe and the Canadiens' beloved Rocket.

Laycoe highsticked Richard in the head, but play continued. Richard turned to the referee, demanding that a penalty be called. He then charged Laycoe, hitting him so hard with his stick that it broke. He picked up another stick and continued his assault, hitting Laycoe in the head and shoulder. As a melee erupted, linesman Cliff Thompson tried to step in, only to be punched in the face by Richard.

The next day, Boston newspapers railed against Richard's conduct. They even claimed that it was Richard, and not Laycoe, who had struck the blow that launched the brawl.

Following a brief inquiry, Richard was suspended until the end of the playoffs, thus costing the Canadiens their best player. Laycoe, on the other hand, received no such sanctions. Habs fans were furious. Rocket Richard was the league's most dynamic player, a natural scorer who played with an unmatched intensity. He was also a revered symbol of French-Canadian sports culture.

Despite the growing discontent in Montreal, Campbell showed up at the Forum on March 17, and sat in his reserved seat. It was a brave move, given the obvious anger simmering in the stands.

The night's contest pitted the Canadiens against the Detroit Red Wings, and by the end of the first period, the Wings were leading 4 to 1. At intermission, the spectators came unglued. They began throwing everything they could find onto the ice, as well as in the direction of Campbell. Suddenly, a loud boom was heard, and the rink filled with clouds of noxious smoke. As security officials tried to evacuate the building, some disgruntled fans violently set upon Campbell.

The riot would rage in the streets of Montreal for more than seven hours. Rioters turned over cars and smashed windows. The next day, Richard made a public statement saying he would accept his suspension and urged fans to get back to cheering the Habs as they began the playoffs.

Some Quebecers considered the suspension of Richard by Clarence Campbell to be an attack on all French Canadians. Did this event help spark a growing sense of nationalism in Quebec? Peut-être!

PART THREE

IN SEARCH OF OURSELVES

1956–1979

Optimism soared like an Avro Arrow as we flew through the fabulous fifties. Progress was our mantra, and a building boom mirrored the baby boom. Armed with picks and spades, we broke ground on a host of nation-building mega-projects. We also set to work creating a uniquely Canadian culture. Gathered around our television sets, we tuned in to CBC Television and gazed at a new generation of homegrown celebrities.

Earlier in the decade, there had been a conflict in Korea that—after two world wars, with countless casualties—left many Canadians feeling an uneasy déjà vu.

On the home front, a different type of crisis was breaking out. War vets who had stared down the Nazis now had their hands full tangling with teenage rebellion. Their kids, born in the lead-up to the Second World War, were talking in a strange slang, greasing their hair, and listening to outrageous new rhythms. When Elvis Presley invaded Toronto in April 1957, the entire country was "All Shook Up."

It had been about fifty years since Prime Minister Wilfrid Laurier's bold prediction that the twentieth century would belong to Canada. We weren't quite there yet—but to many, life seemed picture-perfect.

The 1960s, though, would prove to be a turbulent time—a decade for challenging old assumptions and championing new notions. Did Canadians have a right to health care? Did murderers have a right to live? Canadians faced tough questions without easy answers.

As Canada's centennial neared, we were growing more prosperous and increasingly educated. We still considered ourselves a country of two founding peoples—the British and the French. Our First Nations citizens were left wondering where they fit in that equation.

In truth, we were a nation in search of an identity. Some thought we could find it in symbolism. Perhaps a new flag was the answer? As the sixties grooved on, we wore our hair longer and our pant legs wider. The decade ended with a tide of Trudeaumania and a bold request, made in a Montreal hotel room by one of the world's most famous musicians, to "give peace a chance."

If only it were that easy. Just one year later, Canadians were jolted by terrorist attacks in Quebec and the sight of soldiers patrolling the streets of Ottawa and Montreal.

The seventies would provide Kodak moments in the sport of hockey and the blood sport of politics. It was a time to disco, get fit, and go green. As we bade farewell to the so-called "me decade," Canada stood at a crossroads, its unity soon to be put to the test.

—Mark Reid

51

The Avro Arrow is unveiled, 1957.

A Flying Miracle

Amazing airplane dazzled Canadians

CHRISTOPHER MOORE

This was the happy day. This might have been the best day of the whole program.

On October 4, 1957, RL 201, the first of the Avro Arrows, rolls out into the sunshine and the wide-open skies at Malton, just outside Toronto. There is a stage at left rear, but it stands empty, and the seats in front of it are abandoned. Everyone wants to be close to the star of the show. Everyone just wants to touch the aircraft. Everyone wants to celebrate.

After fifty years of recriminations about what might have been, focus for a moment on the miracle these people saw. This was 1957, remember, just ten years after the breaking of the sound barrier. Lumbering propeller aircraft were still something special.

Here came the Arrow, all straight edges and delta wings, a sleek thing designed for pure and lethal speed far beyond the sound barrier. It was a big aircraft, but twin Iroquois engines nestled at either side of the slim fuselage would transport a crew of two sixteen kilometres high (roughly 53,000 feet) at twice the speed of sound. Instead of manual controls—levers and pulleys—the Arrow employed the fly-by-wire electronics that would become standard twenty-five years later. To this dazzled crowd, the Arrow looked like something that had dropped in from the future.

The Arrow's builders had already produced the CF-100 fighter jet and North America's first commercial passenger jet. They tinkered with a flying car and talked of a supersonic transport, even of spacecraft. They had turned Malton into a humming centre of technology and industry at the forefront of world aviation. Fourteen thousand people worked for Avro directly, another 25,000 in allied industries. By 1957, all their efforts focused on this one plane, a front-line fighter aircraft for the air forces of the Western allies.

Ten thousand people would watch test pilot Jan Zurakowski and RL 201 make a near-perfect first flight of the Arrow in March 1958. RL 201 went supersonic a few days later. Four more Arrows flew that summer and fall. The first Mark 2 Arrow, with the powerful new Iroquois engines the Arrow had been designed for, was ready for taxi trials early in 1959.

But the Arrow's cost, already vast, was rising fast. The strategic situation was fluid. And, really, there never was a chance for any aircraft but an American one to be the key to the West's air defences. In February 1959 came cancellation. The Arrow vanished as if it had never been born. Most of Canada's aviation industry went with it.

So, bad memories surround the Avro Arrow: the cancellation, the blow-torching, the careers blighted, all the bitterness. Better perhaps to recall this moment: thousands of proud Canadians with the beautiful, lethal, world-beating thing they had built together.

Giving Peace a Chance

Nobel win turned Canada into "nation of peacekeepers"

TIM COOK

Justifiably proud, and somewhat surprised, Lester B. Pearson is caught in this 1957 photograph holding his Nobel Peace Prize. Having traded his customary bow tie for a more formal black tie and double-breasted suit, he looks the part of Canada's minister of external affairs. But what could a Canadian minister have done to achieve such international recognition?

Canada was no superpower in the 1950s, although it wanted a deeper involvement in international affairs. Lester B. Pearson—or Mike, as he was generally known—was the most influential Canadian on the world stage. A senior-ranking Canadian diplomat in Britain, the United States, and at the United Nations, Mike had earned the respect of his peers.

Pearson was elected to Parliament in 1948 and was given the external affairs portfolio in Louis St. Laurent's Liberal government. His mettle would be tested in the potential cataclysm of the 1956 Suez Crisis, where he helped to avert a devastating break among the Western allies during one of the most precarious periods of the Cold War.

Egypt's President Gamal Abdel Nasser ached to free his country from its colonial past, but in doing so he had been dangerously playing the Soviets against the Western world in the search for much-needed funds. These brinksmanship politics alienated the West. Nasser further damaged relations when in 1956 he nationalized the Suez Canal. The Suez was a major shipping lane, especially for Western Europe. The British and French were aghast.

These two former great powers conceived a ludicrous plan that involved Israel attacking Egypt, precipitating a crisis that would require the intervention of the French and British, who would then reoccupy the canal. While the Israelis made short work of the Egyptian forces in late October, the Soviet Union—which was in the process of invading Hungary—suddenly threatened massive retaliation. The United States was no happier with the situation, although it wielded economic sanctions rather than the threat of nuclear annihilation.

Something had to be done.

At the United Nations, Mike proposed a peacekeeping force to interpose itself between the two warring sides—and he offered Canadian soldiers to do the job. It was what the world needed, and for his actions Pearson was awarded the Nobel Peace Prize.

This photograph of a proud Pearson seems to capture something beyond his justifiable delight: the small, gold prize quite literally changed the way Canadians viewed themselves, and like a lodestone it dragged Canada out of its warlike orbit and into peace.

Canadians began to think of themselves differently after Pearson's peace force was accepted and then engaged on multiple fronts over the next few decades. The myth of Canada as peacekeeper, especially in relation to our more warlike cousins to the south, remains an enduring one. One wonders what the more than 1.8 million Canadians who served in the six wars of the twentieth century thought of this, or how one squares the welcoming image of the peacekeeper with the 116,000 warriors who died fighting in wars outside of Canada?

52

Lester Pearson displays his Nobel Peace Prize,
Oslo, December 10, 1957.

53

Springhill mine disaster, October 1958.

Disaster in the Depths

Canadians were captivated by coal-mine crisis

PETER MANSBRIDGE

These are two miners in Springhill, Nova Scotia, in October of 1958. Their faces show weariness and despair. The man on the left is covered with coal dust. He is one of the so-called "barefaced" rescue workers, a man who worked without breathing equipment as he dug relentlessly into the Springhill coal mine trying to rescue trapped men.

It was October 23, 1958, just after 8:00 p.m., when the earth shook. The movement is called a "bump," but that is a benign term considering what it did. About four kilometres underground, the floor of the Number 2 mine slammed into the ceiling of the mine. About seventy men were killed instantly. About 100 more were trapped.

The rescue work began immediately, and within twenty-four hours, eighty-one men were led out. But then days went by without any signs of life.

Springhill had known death before at the mine. In 1891, a mine fire had killed 125 men. In 1956, thirty-nine miners were killed in an explosion. Yet, when you say "Springhill mining disaster" today, there is no doubt you are talking about 1958. And there's no doubt why.

The 1958 rescue effort was the first major North American disaster covered on live television. The CBC made its way to Springhill and began telling the world what was happening. There were no small hand-held cameras, no pictures from circling helicopters, no satellite uplinks. It was mostly a reporter talking to rescue workers as they emerged from another shift, pictures of families waiting for news, official statements from company spokesmen. And yet, Canadians—indeed, people around the world—couldn't take their eyes off it.

It was the beginning of our realization that live television would fundamentally change how news was absorbed. Hearing about events wasn't going to cut it anymore. And seeing it the next day wasn't going to be good enough either. This was the perfect TV story—uncomplicated and human. Desperate men above ground trying to reach men entombed below. No one knew if anyone below was alive. Were they crushed? Had they been choked by poisonous gas?

And what an ending. Six days after the bump, rescuers heard voices, and within hours twelve miners were freed. Two days later, seven more men were saved. A barefaced mine rescuer, interviewed by the CBC, said one of the men below had told him he had never given up hope.

Of the 100 survivors, only one later died of his injuries. In the immediate aftermath of the rescue, the ninety-nine "miracles" overshadowed the seventy-five deaths. The story emerged of Maurice Ruddick, a miner who had kept up the morale of the others by singing in the dark. Survivors were invited to New York to be feted on CBS Television's *Ed Sullivan Show*. The town of Springhill was awarded a Carnegie Medal for heroism. An American folksinger wrote "The Ballad of Springhill," later popularized by the group Peter, Paul and Mary.

There was another reality, though. The disaster was enough to convince the Cumberland Railway and Coal Company to shut down the mine once and for all. No matter how heroic all the miners had been, including the two in this photo, they were all out of work.

100 PHOTOS THAT CHANGED CANADA   117

Shakespeare Meets Schmaltz

Duo opened doors for Canadian comedy

JIM BURANT

One of the delights of being a child of the boomer generation—if you were old enough to stay up later, and your family owned a television—was settling down to watch the CBC after Sunday dinner.

At eight o'clock, the CBC—virtually the only channel available to Canadians—would televise the *Ed Sullivan Show*, broadcast from the CBS studios in New York City. It was a weekly entertainment program which could, on any given night, offer high culture in the form of ballet, or opera, as well as low culture, in the form of comedians, jugglers, or puppet shows.

In 1958, though, a new act appeared—Canadian comedians Johnny Wayne and Frank Shuster, or simply Wayne and Shuster. This duo became famous for combining high and low culture in their side-splitting, and occasionally existential, takes on Shakespeare, sports, film noir, and politics.

Frank Shuster and John Weingarten (he later anglicized his name to Wayne) were both born in Toronto, and they met in high school. They each went on to the University of Toronto. From the outset they were born comedians and actors, and they parlayed their experience in varsity productions and the University Follies into jobs working in local radio.

In 1941, they were given their own CBC radio program, called *Shuster & Wayne*. However, the next year they enlisted in the Canadian army and spent most of the Second World War entertaining troops as part of the Canadian Army Show, both in Canada and, after 1944, in overseas theatres. (They would later do the same for the Canadian forces during the Korean conflict.) Upon their demobilization, Wayne and Shuster renewed their career in radio on the CBC in 1946, and entered the world of television in 1954.

Their first appearance on the *Ed Sullivan Show* took place in 1958, at the height of that show's popularity. Watching the show had become a family ritual for millions of Americans, as well as Canadians, in the late 1950s and early 1960s. Wayne and Shuster, in their turn, became part of this phenomenon, setting the record for appearances by any one act on the show—performing sixty-seven times over the next dozen years.

Wayne and Shuster were literate comics, using classical dramas and settings in combination with vaudeville-style slapstick to garner laughs. Their team of bit players and musicians only added to the sophistication of their approach, which won them numerous awards and honours. They influenced a whole generation of comedians in Canada and the United States, and Frank's daughter Rosie was one of the first writers on the iconic U.S. comedy show *Saturday Night Live*, many of whose skits echo the style and wit of Wayne and Shuster.

This photograph, probably taken in 1959 by a CBC staff photographer who accompanied them to New York, shows the duo hamming it up with the show's host, Ed Sullivan.

Johnny Wayne (left) and Frank Shuster (right) with Ed Sullivan, ca. 1958–59.

54

55

A home floats offshore, awaiting high tide, during the Newfoundland outport resettlements in August 1961.

Hope Floats

Outport resettlements painful, but necessary

HON. BRIAN V. TOBIN

Canadians have always been drawn from rural communities to our larger towns and cities. The same is true of Newfoundland and Labrador. However, the pace of resettlement accelerated following Confederation with Canada in 1949, as Premier Joseph Smallwood adopted his policy of "Develop or Perish." Smallwood was determined to bring the newest province of Canada out of poverty and into the mainstream of Canadian society. The traditional inshore fishery was failing, and isolated coastal communites—reliant on the inshore fishery—were often in crisis.

In 1954, Smallwood introduced a voluntary resettlement program and the first of some 300 coastal communities—with over 30,000 men, women, and children—left behind all they knew to start life anew.

Those who could literally severed their homes from their foundations and floated them to their new communities. They took the painful step of abandoning their churches and the graveyards that contained generations of families and friends. They gave up the fishing berths that had been a family birthright and set out across open water to new, larger communities.

The Smallwood government had promised a better life for all Newfoundlanders. However, while the voluntary resettlement programs attracted many, they were not enough.

By 1965, new measures were introduced. It had been sixteen years since Confederation, and both the provincial and federal governments were struggling to provide medical, educational, and transportation services to isolated coastal communities. The new federal-provincial Fisheries Household Resettlement Program required communities to vote on whether to take part; to negotiate the terms of their resettlement; and to then vote again before qualifying for compensation.

Entire communities were moved to growth centres where new jobs in the deep-sea fishery, in fish plants, and in service industries were said to be waiting. Although many jobs were promised, not all were delivered, and the resettlement program proved to be deeply controversial. To this day, the debate continues; much of the literature, poetry, theatre, and music of Newfoundland and Labrador is influenced by the resettlement programs.

The question is: Was resettlement a boon or a bane to the people of the province? Many of resettlement's harshest critics have never lived in the outport communities that often lacked water and sewer services, adequate education facilities, or life-saving basic health care.

In this 1961 photo, three children watch as a home belonging to Malcolm Rogers is moored offshore, awaiting high tide. When Rogers floated his home from Silver Fox Island to Dover, on Bonavista Bay, his heart must have been heavy for all that he had left behind. However, it's equally true that in painfully breaking with the past, Rogers had improved his children's future. Rogers had done what generations of Canadians have done—sailed across a bay, or across an ocean, to secure brighter futures for the generations that followed.

Bad Medicine

Medicare sparked fevered debate across Canada

DON NEWMAN

The weather was hot. So were tempers. Saskatchewan had never seen anything like it. Nor had any other place else in Canada.

It was the summer of 1962, and doctors in the province had withdrawn their services to protest a radical new government health insurance plan. Those in favour of—and those against—"medicare" had gathered by the hundreds at the provincial legislature to voice their anger.

In a provincial election two years earlier, the left-leaning Co-operative Commonwealth Federation government, led by T.C. "Tommy" Douglas, had promised a government health insurance plan. After winning its fifth majority in sixteen years, the CCF managed to pass its medicare bill.

It was not without controversy, though. During the election campaign, the other parties had opposed medicare. But, more important, so had the Saskatchewan College of Physicians and Surgeons. And the doctors weren't alone—physicians across Canada and the United States were determined to block what they called "socialized medicine" in North America—because, if medicare was introduced and worked in Saskatchewan, why not everywhere else, too?

Douglas had led the CCF since 1944. While he was a driving force behind medicare, he left the party before it was implemented. In the summer of 1961, Douglas was elected the first leader of the federal New Democratic Party. He stepped down as premier with ten months to go before medicare came into effect. As the July 1, 1962, medicare deadline approached, doctors ramped up their campaign against it. They predicted dire consequences if the plan went ahead. Just how dire, they didn't immediately announce. Soon, however, the doctors agreed to withdraw their services on the day medicare came into effect. The province began negotiations, but by the evening of June 30, no solution was in sight. The next day, Saskatchewan's doctors walked out.

The eyes of the world were suddenly on the province. And for the next three weeks, a war of words was waged. Labour unions and the CCF political machine supported the government. Opposition parties launched campaigns in support of the doctors. Rallies were held, and ads, both for and against medicare, hit the airwaves. Saskatchewan residents, meanwhile, just tried not to get sick or injured.

After three weeks of chaos, sanity returned. A face-saving deal for the doctors allowed the medicare plan to go into effect as planned. Fortunately, the strike claimed no lives. But there were other victims.

The first was Tommy Douglas. The federal election was held just three weeks before medicare was to come into effect, and he went down to defeat. He would have to move to British Columbia to resurrect his political career. In 1964, the CCF government was defeated after twenty years in power. But when it returned to power eight years later—this time as an NDP government—every province in Canada had a version of Saskatchewan's medicare system.

Regina medicare strike, July 1962.

57

Protesters crying during Canada's last executions, 1962

Crimes and Punishments

Did scenes of sorrow help end capital punishment?

NELLE OOSTEROM

The weeping woman in this photo was part of a group of demonstrators who stood in bitter cold outside Toronto's Don Jail on December 10, 1962, shortly before the last executions were carried out in Canada. They were polite, neatly dressed—not the sort of long-haired hippies who would come to dominate protest movements of all kinds in just a few years. And their small numbers belied the strong support they had for their cause—the abolition of capital punishment.

Even Prime Minister John Diefenbaker was on their side.

"I know what it means to sign a death warrant," Diefenbaker would later say in 1975. "I've concluded that innocent men can be executed and have been executed."

Diefenbaker's stance was personal. As a defence lawyer in Saskatchewan, he said he saw one of his clients wrongfully executed for a murder he didn't commit. Diefenbaker's Conservative government had commuted no less than fifty-two of sixty-six death sentences by the time this picture was taken. Abolition of capital punishment was seen as imminent.

In fact, the federal cabinet discussed commuting the death sentences of Arthur Lucas and Ronald Turpin. There was doubt about their convictions—Turpin was seen by some to be mentally unstable and Lucas, who had an IQ in the low 60s, was convicted almost entirely on circumstantial evidence. Yet politicians nevertheless decided to go ahead with the hangings of Turpin, who shot a policeman to death, and Lucas, who was convicted of killing an FBI informant in Toronto. Their deaths shortly after midnight on December 11, 1962, brought the number of people hanged in Canada to 710.

Canadians did not come by their anti-death-penalty stance overnight. A private member's bill had called for abolition in 1914, but it was shelved. With the postwar optimism of the 1950s came new reforms; and in every parliamentary session between 1954 and 1963, a private member's bill called for abolition. Finally, in 1966—four years after Turpin and Lucas were hanged—the government passed Bill C-168, which limited capital murder to the killing of police and prison guards. A decade later, in a free vote in the House of Commons, Canada abolished capital punishment altogether for civilian offences. The military retained its right to execute personnel—but that too passed into history in 1998 with a rewrite of the National Defence Act.

But the debate is not over. As recently as 1987, there was an unsuccessful motion in the House of Commons to reintroduce the death penalty. And protestors today are more likely to weep for the victims of crime. Yet, the arguments put forward by these well-mannered demonstrators back in 1962 have proven themselves over time: The repeal of capital punishment did not lead to an increase in the homicide rate. And conviction rates for first-degree murder doubled in the decade following abolition—suggesting that it's easier for jury members to convict for murder if they know they are not sending someone to their death.

The Great Flag Debate

Flag flap showed symbols matter

WILL FERGUSON

A boisterous crowd rallies in 1964 to show their support for the "Pearson Pennant": three red maple leaves, bordered by blue. Our national flag is visible in this prototypical design. What is more significant, however, is what is *not* shown: no Union Jack, no fleurs-de-lis, no reference whatsoever to the country's founding European nations.

The flag these young men are celebrating, like the final version it would morph into, is one stripped of imperial overtones, of any mention of Canada's colonial past. The roots of this lie in an earlier crisis and the stinging rebuff received by a Canadian diplomat.

In 1956, Egypt nationalized the Suez Canal, and Britain and France responded by bombing the Canal Zone. As the crisis quickly escalated to the brink of world war, Canada's foreign minister, Lester Pearson, stepped in. He proposed a system of "peacekeepers"—neutral armies that would step in between antagonists and maintain a ceasefire until a truce could be arranged.

The plan worked and the Third World War was averted. Pearson would go on to win the Nobel Peace Prize for his efforts, but when it came time to mobilize the United Nation's first peacekeeping force, Egypt refused to allow Canadian soldiers to be involved. How could Canada claim to be a disinterested participant, the president of Egypt wanted to know, when its uniform was still that of the British Army and its flag still featured a Union Jack in one corner?

Pearson had learned an important lesson: national symbols matter; they are the clearest message of national character. And when Pearson became the prime minister in 1963 he quickly set out to give Canada a flag of its own, one free of any colonial overtones or Old World connections.

The new design was based on the emblem of Kingston's Military College and was put forward by historian George F. G. Stanley. The maple leaf itself was a historic Canadian symbol, one that can be traced back to the 1700s. In the War of 1812, nationalist mythology has it that the French and English Canadians who held back an American invasion at the Battle of Chateauguay had camouflaged themselves with sprigs of red maple. By the First World War, Canadian soldiers were identified by their maple leaf badges, and by 1960 even the Royal Canadian Legion had adopted it as its symbol.

It was a contentious choice, nonetheless, and the "Great Flag Debates" of 1964 were known for their vitriolic nature. While many viewed it as an important step in Canada's ongoing evolution, others were just as adamant the new flag represented an erosion of national values. They saw it as an affront, a denial of the country's British heritage. The flag debates ended loudly, with Pearson's Liberals rising to sing "O Canada!" and Diefenbaker's Conservatives replying with their own defiant rendition of "God Save the Queen!"

On February 15, 1965, Canada's new national flag—a single red maple leaf on a field of white, bordered by red bars—was raised for the first time above the Peace Tower in Ottawa.

58

Supporters of the "Pearson Pennant" rally on Parliament Hill, 1964.

Ku Klux Klan members from Georgia on *This Hour Has Seven Days*, October 24, 1965.

Must-See TV
Provocative program was too good to last
PETER DESBARATS

59

Sunday evening, October 4, 1964, saw the debut of what has been called the most exciting and influential program in the history of Canadian television—*This Hour Has Seven Days*. It was a unique hour-long amalgam of news, documentaries, comedy, satire, and whatever else its producers decided to show on that particular weekend.

Seven Days, as it was usually called, was launched when Canadian television itself was only twelve years old. There had been other documentary and public affairs shows on Canadian TV, but none had the immediate and spectacular impact of *Seven Days*. This was largely due to two visionaries, Patrick Watson and Douglas Leiterman, who intuitively sensed the role of television as the most powerful news medium of our day.

For two gripping seasons, *Seven Days* enthralled the country. Everyone watched it, and talked about it the next day. No political topic or public figure was safe. Its second program coincided with the Queen's visit to Canada; *Seven Days* portrayed her as a cockney housewife in curlers delivering the annual Christmas message. The show's second season opened with a skit featuring the Pope, played by a *Seven Days* journalist. And then there were jaw-dropping moments, such as the unrehearsed 1965 studio confrontation between two leaders of the Ku Klux Klan and Reverend Jim Bevel, a Martin Luther King disciple, moderated by Robert Hoyt of *Seven Days*. As this photo shows, *Seven Days* was willing to push the definition of "acceptable" television—and Canadians were transfixed.

It was all too good—or perhaps too bad, as some would have it—to last. As controversy mounted over the show's content, CBC brass decided to pull the plug. A public outcry ensued, prompting a parliamentary committee hearing and the appointment of a special investigator to probe the decision. Some CBC managers resigned in protest, but the show's fate was sealed. After its final program on May 8, 1966, *Seven Days* began to slip slowly into history—but its achievements remained an influential example.

For the first and probably the only time, Canadians were involved passionately from coast to coast in a debate about the survival of a single television program. The questions remain topical today: How do you define "good" television journalism? How do you produce it? Is it possible to have a "free" press in the new electronic media? What is the role of political satire in this new multimedia world?

Today, edgy shows, such as the CBC's *Rick Mercer Report,* continue to blur the lines of the "newsmagazine" genre. Is it political commentary, or satirical entertainment? However defined, it and others of its ilk all carry some of the genetic material of *Seven Days*. And Canadians remain transfixed.

Built for Show

Amazing Expo wowed the world

CHRISTOPHER MOORE

This was not Expo 67. When they took this photograph in 1965, they were still building the place. Still, there was an honest promise here of what Expo would offer: pretty girls and kick-ass design. It was going to be a show with legs.

They started late, only after Moscow dropped its claim to the world's fair for 1967. Governments dithered and changed. Few Canadians believed it could work, or work on time.

Design saved the fair. Construction was built on a critical path—everything would be ready just when it was needed, not a moment sooner. For the first few years, the site in Montreal was all mud. That's because most of the fair stood on new islands made of rock and dirt dumped into the fast-flowing river. The skins of buildings and the landscaping were the very last elements on the critical path, and were completed just before the opening.

What to show the world in the meantime? Design again saved the day. Build "Expo 67" in monumental letters, cheap and quick and memorable as the pyramids. Then surround them with pretty girls. In the late 1960s, the miniskirt's power to tease and thrill was right at its apex. Organizers likely thought: This could be the photograph that will sell a million package tours.

Fortunately, Montreal's world fair for 1967 delivered on its promise and more. Canada's pride was saved, and soon, relief turned to delight. *Terre des Hommes* tapped the sixties' sudden flowering of secular humanist optimism: creativity, technology, and global connections all seemed benign and full of promise. It was a wonderful world to walk around in, and it said that if we designed things right, we could do anything.

In 1967, the world seemed ready for a great world's fair. Fifty million people came, more than anyone expected, more than had ever attended a world's fair before. As the people flowed in, they liked what they saw. The buildings of Expo turned out to be the most exciting architectural collection anyone had seen. There were geodesic domes and inverted pyramids, fifteen-storey tents full of air and space, and hulking grids of iron girders. Every avenue and plaza was a riot of experimentation in form and colour, all designed to amaze and delight and challenge. And in a landscape designed for pleasure and enjoyment, everyone was young and beautiful and bilingual. All the hostesses seemed to be as blonde and leggy as the cheerleader in the foreground.

Soon after the fair's six months were up, the visiting officials sent their spectacular displays back to their home countries. They tore down most of the amazing buildings, for few of them were built to withstand the winter. It was as if Expo 67 had been all an illusion after all—like the photograph. But what a magical illusion it had been!

60

ex

expo67

PASSPORT
TO MAN AND HIS WORLD
ADULTE – ADULT

Expo 67 promotion, Montreal, 1965

61

Charles de Gaulle speaks in
Montreal, July 24, 1967.

Vive le Québec libre!

Famous declaration inflamed passions in Quebec and Canada

JACQUES LACOURSIÈRE

Montreal was buzzing as it prepared to host Expo 67, the world fair that would be the centre-piece of Canada's centennial celebrations.

Many world leaders planned to visit Canada and to attend Expo 67, including Charles de Gaulle, the president of France. Protocol dictated that de Gaulle should begin his official visit at Ottawa—but the French president had other ideas.

In a surprising move, the Quebec delegate general in Paris proposed that de Gaulle's official visit would be made by boat and not by plane, allowing him to sail directly up the St. Lawrence River to Quebec.

On July 23, 1967, the *Colbert* arrived at Quebec City and docked at L'Anse au Foulon. Roland Michener, the new governor general of Canada, welcomed the French president, beginning a series of official ceremonies.

No one knew that de Gaulle was secretly setting the stage for the now-famous declaration he would eventually make in Montreal. He dropped hints of what was to come during a banquet at the historic Château Frontenac, saying in French: "Here we are witnessing, as in many regions of the world, the emancipation of a people who, in every respect, want self-determination and control over their destinies."

The next day, de Gaulle and his entourage made a triumphant parade through the province, stopping several times to greet Quebecers as he made his way to Montreal.

By this time, more than 25,000 people had gathered to await de Gaulle's arrival. The French president wasn't scheduled to speak, but what de Gaulle wants, he gets! Standing on a balcony at Montreal's city hall, he told the crowd that France was watching "what was happening" in Quebec and ended his rousing speech with these now-famous words: "Vive Montréal! Vive le Québec! Vive le Québec libre!"

Pierre Bourgault, at the time the president of Quebec's main sovereignist movement, was unable to mask his enthusiasm. He told a reporter from *Paris Match* that "for seven years I have been shouting the same slogan in Quebec, but few listened. De Gaulle comes here, says it only once and the whole world listens."

Back in Ottawa, there was outrage. Conservative Party Leader John Diefenbaker accused the federal government of being irresponsible for allowing de Gaulle to make his incendiary comments. Prime Minister Lester Pearson, also angry with de Gaulle, responded, "Canadians do not need to be liberated."

As criticism erupted both in Canada and in France, de Gaulle cut his trip short and returned home without ever visiting Ottawa. Upon his return, de Gaulle declared of the sovereignist movement: "I have furthered their cause by ten years!"

The Culling Fields

Images from the ice fuelled anti-sealing sentiment

TINA LOO

"The Revolution is just a T-shirt away," observed folk singer Billy Bragg. In St. John's, Newfoundland, and Labrador, they certainly think so. One hip store gives customers the opportunity to wear their politics, declaring themselves "Bay Girls" (and Boys) or members of the "Newfoundland Liberation Army." Tourists often snap the shirts up, but even the most enthusiastic buyer might pause before plunking down thirty dollars for a local best-seller, one proclaiming "I ♣ Baby Seals."

Sealing has been part of Newfoundland's history for much longer than the province has been a part of Canada. The hunt started in the early decades of the eighteenth century, and by the end of the nineteenth century sealing was one of the colony's most important industries, second only to the cod fishery.

Particularly before the mid-twentieth century, the life of a sealer could be nasty, brutish, and short: perhaps not too far removed from that of his quarry, the harp seal. Sealing was the stuff of legend: One hundred years ago a photo like this would have been read very differently—especially in Newfoundland—as emblematic of the hardship and heroism of a people that wrested a living from the land.

For many people, however, this is a picture of cruelty, of gratuitous violence meted out to innocent animals. In the hands of media-savvy environmentalists, images like this one were "mind bombs"—weapons mightier than the hakapik—which brought groups like the International Fund for Animal Welfare and Greenpeace the attention and money they needed, even after the killing of whitecoats was banned.

Although the Canadian government began to regulate the hunt in the 1960s, its actions did little to persuade protesters that any bloodshed at all was justified. Everything about sealing was contested, from its sustainability and economic importance to the ethics of wearing fur and the cruelty of the hunt.

CBC personality and Newfoundlander Rex Murphy once called the protesters "astronauts of stupidity," but facts couldn't counter the power of images. The sealers weren't as cute as the seals. In 1982, the European Economic Community banned the importation of seal pup skins, dealing a blow to the industry. By the nineties, both the seal hunt and cod fishery had collapsed, leaving the province in desperate straits.

Pictures like this one marked an evolution in the sophistication and reach of the environmental movement. Powerful enough to change how people saw their relationship to other creatures, they were responsible for furthering the cause of animal rights globally.

For Newfoundlanders, such photos didn't so much mark a change as signal a troubling extension of the separation of interests and understanding that exists between Newfoundland and the rest of the world. Whether it was Brigitte Bardot in the 1970s or Paul McCartney in 2006, Newfoundlanders might be excused if they saw the gnashing of celebrity teeth as just the latest expression of a colonial mentality that stretches back a century.

62

Canadian seal hunter, 1969.

63

John Lennon and Yoko Ono's bed-in for peace, Montreal, May 1969.

Starting a Revolution

"Bed-in" in Canada changed the world

THOMAS S. AXWORTHY

Canada was cool in 1969.

John Lennon's eight-day bed-in for peace at the Queen Elizabeth Hotel in Montreal, from May 26 to June 2—captured evocatively in Ted Church's photograph from the *Montreal Gazette*—was one of the seminal events of that era.

Many will view the photo with a wry grin—remembering the idealism, creativity, and craziness of the event, and the decade it typified. Others will frown and agree with conservative historian Gertrude Himmelfarb that the sixties counterculture was "an adversary culture" ruined by "unrestrained individualism."

"In many ways it was a glorious interlude," writes George Perry in *London in the Sixties*, "a moment of release when the teacher leaves the room and the class realizes it is on temporary license." The ringleader of this unruly class was John Winston Lennon of Liverpool, the most iconic member of the most iconic rock band ever—the Beatles. The baby boom generation and the Beatles are entwined in a love affair that has never faltered.

In 1969, Lennon married Yoko Ono, an avant-garde artist, and the two used their celebrity status to promote world peace as the war in Vietnam fearsomely escalated. Taking to their bed in suite 1738–1742, Lennon became the first rocker to urge his global following to take a political stand. The media eagerly responded, and spread the Lennon happening worldwide.

In an interview, Lennon said, "Give peace a chance!" As the phrase resonated, he began to compose the verses that eventually became the most powerful anti-war anthem in history. Joined by fifty celebrities and supporters, Lennon ordered recording equipment and, from his bed in the early hours of June 1, "Give Peace a Chance" was born. Only months later, at the Vietnam moratorium of November 15, 1969, a half-million demonstrators were singing the song in front of the Washington Monument.

Canada was not simply incidental to the bed-in story. Denied entry to the United States, Lennon visited Canada three times in 1969. When many had soured on the activist Beatle, Canadians, including Prime Minister Pierre Trudeau, were welcoming. Lennon praised Canada for not "interfering in foreign countries." The well-known group chorus of Lennon's famous song was sung largely by Canadians.

Alas, if only we had listened. Wars continue, and Lennon himself was a victim of the violence he abhorred. But his ideals endure. At age sixteen, Gail Renard, now a noted television writer, used her university press card to get past the security guards. Her first published piece was "Eight Days in Montreal with John and Yoko." Because she helped Lennon transcribe his lyrics, he later gave his originals to her. In remembering that extraordinary week, she speaks for her generation: "Thanks to John . . . I became braver. It made me think you can change the world, or at least your bit of it, and you should always try to."

Desperate Measures

Canadians were startled by soldiers on the streets

DESMOND MORTON

Long before Americans endured the 9/11 attacks of 2001, Canadians were gripped by their own terrorist crisis. On October 5, 1970, a Front de libération du Québec cell kidnapped James Cross, the British trade representative in Montreal. The next morning, Canadians awoke to a communiqué from the terrorist group: Unless both Ottawa and Montreal obeyed a series of FLQ demands, Cross would die. Although federal officials reacted angrily, on October 8, the FLQ's radical manifesto was read in deadpan fashion by a Radio-Canada newsreader.

Two days later, as Quebec Premier Robert Bourassa returned from a trade mission to New York, Parti Québécois leader René Lévesque appealed to the FLQ to shun violence. That night, Quebec's labour minister, Pierre Laporte, was seized outside his suburban home as his wife and children watched in horror.

Laporte's kidnapping sparked what is now known as the October Crisis. In Ottawa, the federal government summoned soldiers to protect government ministers and key buildings. In Quebec, excited crowds of students and labour militants gathered to cheer any spasm of radicalism.

On October 13, Prime Minister Pierre Trudeau encountered two TV journalists who questioned whether the government was overreacting. "There are a lot of bleeding hearts around who just don't like to see people with helmets and guns," he told them. "All I can say is: go on and bleed. . . ." How far would he go, they asked? "Well, just watch me" was Trudeau's terse reply.

Bourassa's officials, meanwhile, had explored emergency legislation and recommended that the federal government use the War Measures Act (WMA), invented in 1914 and last applied in 1939. On October 15, Bourassa called out for Canadian soldiers "in aid of the civil power." On October 26, Trudeau imposed the WMA, claiming that Bourassa and Montreal mayor Jean Drapeau had supplied "conclusive evidence that insurrection, real or apprehended, exists and has existed." NDP leader Tommy Douglas protested the decision. Polls, meanwhile, showed 92 per cent of Canadians were in favour of the move.

Thousands of soldiers deployed to Quebec, Montreal, and Ottawa, freeing police to hunt for the kidnap victims and to arrest suspects. Within forty-eight hours, 250 Quebecers were behind bars, including union leaders, entertainers, writers, and PQ supporters. By month's end, 1,628 raids had swept up 400 suspects.

Montrealers looked with apprehension upon sights such as this soldier—a member of the Royal 22nd Regiment—guarding a light helicopter. What if these youngsters decided to push past the soldier? Would he fire his rifle or merely beat them off? Would he be blamed if a child was hurt or even killed?

Over time, memories of the October Crisis faded. So did public approval of the WMA. René Lévesque won his fight to make Quebec sovereignty an issue decided by votes, not violence. Scenes like the one in this photograph are familiar in countries where Canadians are sent to keep the peace. Thoughtful Canadians should rejoice that they are a rarity here.

64

The War Measures Act, Montreal, October 16, 1970.

... prepared to ...
... aves by a free society, operating by its ...
society open on the world. Our struggle can o...
people that has awakened cannot long be kept ...

Long live Free Quebec!
Long live our comrades the political prisoner...
Long live the Quebec Revoluti...
Long live the Front de L...

The body of Pierre Laporte is discovered, October 17, 1970.

65

A Terrible Turning Point

Grisly discovery horrified Canadians

JACQUES LACOURSIÈRE

Just before midnight on Saturday, October 17, 1970, Quebec provincial police opened the trunk of a car and found the body of Pierre Laporte, the minister of labour in Quebec Premier Robert Bourassa's cabinet.

The previous Saturday, Laporte had been abducted by members of the Chenier cell. This was the second abduction by the Front de libération du Québec, also known as the FLQ; the first kidnapping had taken place on the morning of October 5. That victim, James Richard Cross, was Britain's trade commissioner to Montreal. The FLQ had also claimed responsibility for Cross's abduction.

In their first communiqué, the FLQ cell listed seven conditions that had to be met before they would release their hostage. A few days later, the FLQ members revised their list of initial demands down to three: broadcast of their manifesto; a halt to police investigations of the FLQ; and the release of all "political" prisoners in Quebec.

The kidnappings were the latest in a string of terrorist actions in Quebec dating back to 1963. The FLQ had launched mail bomb attacks at numerous targets, including federal government sites and in the largely anglophone area of Montreal known as Westmount. Later, certain cells targeted companies they considered to be "exploiters" of the working class. In 1969, the Montreal stock exchange was forced to close its public gallery following an FLQ attack.

The kidnappings in 1970 came at a particularly turbulent time in Quebec. The Quebec government was also facing a general strike by specialist doctors, and there was a growing sense of concern in the province. Events would spiral, leading to the federal government's declaration of the War Measures Act and the arrest of hundreds of Quebecers.

Around 7 p.m. on October 17, a communiqué was sent to a radio station declaring that Laporte had been "liquidated." However, it wasn't until shortly before midnight that the trunk of the car containing the minister's body was opened.

The murder of Laporte shocked and horrified both Quebecers and Canadians throughout the country. After newspapers published the grisly photo of Laporte's body, many Quebecers who had earlier sympathized with the goals—if not the methods—of the FLQ distanced themselves from the terrorist group. FLQ members Paul Rose and Francis Simard were eventually arrested, tried, and found guilty of Laporte's murder. Other cell members were captured and convicted either of kidnapping, or of being an accessory to Laporte's abduction.

As for James Cross, he was released unharmed in early December, effectively ending the October Crisis. The impacts of this turning point in Canadian history continue to be felt today.

Making Waves

Eco-group rode rising tide of environmentalism

TINA LOO

Not long after this photo was snapped, the world came to know these men as the Rainbow Warriors. The name matched their sartorial choices, as it did the varied influences that coloured the politics of the group they founded.

A coalition of "mystics and mechanics," Greenpeace drew on the counterculture, the New Left, ecology, and the peace movement for its ideas. From its humble beginnings in Vancouver, it grew into an international organization with 2.8 million supporters and offices in forty-one countries. Despite its name, environmental issues weren't its initial focus. Concerned about nuclear testing by the United States in the Aleutian Islands, Jim Bohlen and Irving Stowe, two American expatriates, founded the Don't Make a Wave Committee in 1969.

For a while, it looked as if the new committee would be swamped by the ideological cross-currents of its own membership. No one could agree on what the group would actually *do* until Bohlen and his wife Marie brought up the Quaker idea of bearing witness. The committee would find a ship and sail north to "confront the bomb."

The *Phyllis Cormack*, rechristened the *Greenpeace*, set off with its Rainbow Warriors for Amchitka in 1971. When the North Pacific proved too much for the old halibut seiner, the group turned back 1,400 kilometres short of its destination, opting instead to make a series of coastal whistle stops on the way back to Vancouver to raise awareness about the nuclear threat.

Despite their failure to stop the tests, the crew considered the voyage a success. Due to the publicity it had garnered, Canadians from coast to coast began demonstrating for peace. The rising tide of sentiment against the detonations led the United States to abandon further testing at Amchitka. Rebranding themselves the Greenpeace Foundation, the members of the Don't Make a Wave Committee continued bearing witness to weapons testing, taking on the French in the South Pacific.

Influenced by ecologists, in the mid-1970s the organization shifted its attention, undertaking campaigns against commercial whaling in the Pacific and the Newfoundland seal hunt. Although its targets were different, the tactics were the same: direct confrontation and shrewd use of the media. While these campaigns raised the profile of the Vancouver organization, they cost a lot of money. Debt became a problem which could be solved only by the creation of Greenpeace International in 1979. While the Vancouver group had its debt paid by Greenpeace's European affiliates, it was forced to cede control to this global organization.

Many accuse the founders of Greenpeace of selling out, of going from confronting "the man" to being the man, of trading their plaid shirts and peace signs for button-downs and business cards. But that assumes Greenpeace was wholly idealistic from the start. Given the heady mix of ideologies that was present from its beginnings, "compromised idealism" was always at the heart of the Don't Make a Wave movement. In that sense, Greenpeace was—and remains—Canadian.

Greenpeace's first mission, Vancouver, B.C., September 1971.

Viola Léger as *La Sagouine*, November 26, 1971.

Acadian Odyssey

Acadia's past, present collided at play's debut

DR. ROBERT PICHETTE

"It ain't easy to make a life for yourself when you don't even have your own country to live in, and you can't tell nobody what nationality you are. You end up not having the faintest idea who you are any more."

These lines are spoken during the astonishing soliloquy *La Sagouine*, created by the renowned author Antonine Maillet. And for generations, these lines reflected the feelings of the descendants of the roughly 15,000 Acadians who were expelled in the 1750s from what became the Maritime provinces.

However, by the time this photograph was taken at the Université de Moncton in November 1971—at the debut performance of *La Sagouine*—Acadians were no longer a diffident lot. Rather, they had embarked on a stunning cultural revival that remodelled their society, particularly in New Brunswick, and *La Sagouine*—the story of a wise Acadian washerwoman from the wrong side of the tracks—was talking about a very dead past.

The Expulsion was devastating to the Acadian people. Those who managed to return to Acadia found their former homes occupied by their oppressors. The Acadians would endure generations of hardship as they eked out a living on the fringes of New Brunswick, Nova Scotia, and Prince Edward Island.

By the 1970s, however, the Acadians had largely laid the past to rest, thanks to the efforts of a new vanguard of Acadian political, cultural, and intellectual leadership. Much was owed to Liberal Louis J. Robichaud, the first Acadian to be elected premier of New Brunswick. During his years in power, from 1960 to 1970, he thoroughly modernized the governance of the province, making it officially bilingual in the process, with the full backing of his eventual successor, Progressive Conservative Richard Hatfield. After years in the wilderness, Acadians were finally being welcomed into positions of power.

When Viola Léger, an educator turned actress, first played the role of *La Sagouine*, the Université de Moncton was just eight years old. It quickly became the intellectual centre of the new Acadia. Many Acadians connected to the university would go on to achieve greatness: Léger would be appointed to the Canadian Senate; Maillet, who won France's coveted Prix Goncourt in 1979, served as the school's chancellor; so did Roméo LeBlanc, the long-serving federal politician who became the first Acadian governor general of Canada. Forty-six years after its foundation in 1963, the university boasts more than 42,000 graduates, many of them Acadians who today have a very good idea of who they are.

La Sagouine includes this line: "You're part of a country, maybe, but you have no place in it." That's no longer true. Looking back, it seems right and proper that the world premiere of *La Sagouine* was staged at the Université de Moncton in 1971, if only to provide a scale of comparison between the dreadful past and the vibrant Acadian present—and, no doubt, equally bright future.

Henderson's Goal

Last-minute salvation for hockey-mad nation

CHRIS WEBB

This is what redemption looks like—but it didn't come easy.

When news hit in April 1972 that Canada's greatest hockey pros would challenge the Soviet Union to an eight-game "Friendship Series," the entire country knew it would be anything but friendly.

For years, the Soviets had dominated the international amateur game. But now our top stars were taking to the ice and hockey fans salivated at the thought of Canada's best sweeping the Big Red Machine.

The series opened in Montreal with no one expecting a Soviet victory. Canadians believed the Communists would crumble against the likes of Phil Esposito and Bobby Clarke.

They were wrong. Game 1 ended in a 7-3 victory for the Soviets, sending shock waves throughout Canada. The Canadians bounced back for a win in Toronto and then a tie in Winnipeg. But in Game 4, fans booed the home team off the ice after a 5-3 loss in Vancouver. "This isn't a game. This is a war and we'd better get ourselves together," Esposito, Canada's captain, said at the time.

This was a Cold War of flashing skates and crushing bodychecks. Two ideologies—opposing ways of life and of playing hockey—fought for supremacy.

The shaky home series left many Canadians unsure of Canada's status as a great hockey nation. The unsteadiness worsened when the series shifted to Moscow, where the Canucks lost Game 5 and barely won Games 6 and 7.

On September 28, 1972, Canadians everywhere gathered anxiously around their TVs and radios for the eighth and final game of the series.

In the dying seconds at Moscow's Luzhniki Sports Palace—with the score tied at 5-5—Paul Henderson flew into the Soviet zone, shooting once, getting the rebound, and then shooting again. Foster Hewitt, the voice of Canadian hockey, shouted the words that still leave the hearts of many Canadians racing: "Henderson has scored for Canada!"

Henderson raised his arms in the air and was embraced by teammate Yvon Cournoyer, while goalie Vladislav Tretiak lay sprawled in defeat behind them. Canadian fans leapt from their seats.

For many Canadians, it is the single greatest sporting moment of their lives. The roar of celebration in the streets and living rooms across Canada was about more than hockey. For a country sometimes divided by language and identity, millions came together to support what has been called the greatest hockey team of the twentieth century.

This immortal image, photographed by the *Toronto Star's* Frank Lennon, has since been reproduced as a coin, a postage stamp, and on countless hockey cards and posters.

The Summit Series remains one of the few athletic events that transcended Canadian sport to become part of our collective consciousness.

68

Paul Henderson celebrates after scoring against the Soviets, September 28, 1972.

69

Prime Minister Pierre Trudeau with son, Justin, August 10, 1973

Love-Hate Leader

Iconic and enigmatic, Trudeau still fascinates

PETER DESBARATS

Pierre Elliott Trudeau was a harried, but young-looking father when he hoisted his first-born, Justin, on his hip to receive this RCMP salute. In fact, he was in his fifties, an age when many men are entering grandfatherhood.

Trudeau was fifty-two in 1971 when he married twenty-two-year-old Margaret Sinclair. It was typical of the way Canada's fifteenth prime minister ignored the calendar. When Trudeau was a serious young student in Montreal, he tended to act old for his age. But as he grew older, eventually fathering three sons and a daughter, he seemed to undergo a kind of delayed adolescence—and so did many normally staid Canadians. It was all part of what became known as Trudeaumania, and you either loved it or couldn't stand it. Quebec separatists, for instance, hated him with a passion felt almost as equally in the hearts of some Western Canadians.

Back in the 1940s, though, no one could have imagined the spectacular future that lay in store for Trudeau—or the radical transformation that was about to occur in Quebec. Almost overnight, it transformed itself from a rural-based, conservative society to an urban and increasingly radical population. Returning home in the 1960s from doctoral studies in the United States, London and Paris, Trudeau was still relatively unknown outside Quebec. He considered himself a socialist, but was convinced to run for the federal Liberals in the 1965 election. As a cabinet minister under Lester Pearson, Trudeau introduced legislation to decriminalize homosexual acts between consenting adults and to legalize contraception.

During the 1968 election, Trudeau's flair for the dramatic produced a hugely symbolic event. He was in Montreal for the St-Jean-Baptiste Day parade when separatists started throwing rocks and bottles at the reviewing stand. Despite the danger, Trudeau refused to take cover. The television image of Trudeau standing up to the separatists clinched the election for him when it was held the following day.

Now suddenly prime minister, Trudeau successfully appeared to turn the clock back. His political and personal styles had always verged on the flamboyant. As a bachelor, he dated celebrities; during overseas trips, he once slid down a Buckingham Palace banister and, in 1977, famously pirouetted behind the Queen's back.

The longer he was in office, though, the more difficult became the political challenges. The national debt grew dramatically, and Trudeau infuriated Westerners with a national energy program. His perceived arrogance—the other side of the intellectual brilliance—eroded his popularity. But there also were triumphs during his two terms in office, from 1968 to 1979 and from 1980 to 1984: the implementation of official bilingualism; the patriation of the Canadian Constitution, and the creation of the Charter of Rights and Freedoms.

His death in September 2000 was met with an unprecedented outpouring of public grief. Almost a decade later, we are still trying to decipher the enigma that was Pierre Trudeau. As his biographers, Stephen Clarkson and Christina McCall once wrote, "He haunts us still."

A Political Fumble

Infamous photo-op ushered in era of image politics

CHRIS WEBB

Let it be a lesson to politicians staging photo ops: All it takes is one wrong move—or in this case, a fumbled football—to break you.

Robert Stanfield discovered this truism the hard way while on the campaign trail in 1974. Although he never had the same flair as his Liberal rival, Pierre Trudeau, many Progressive Conservative supporters regarded Stanfield as a strong and inspiring leader. He supported official bilingualism, even though it was unpopular to do so, and he succeeded in uniting the party after the turbulent Diefenbaker years.

Stanfield had just missed becoming Canada's fifteenth prime minister in 1972, losing to Trudeau by a two-seat margin. Two years later, he felt ready for a rematch.

In the 1974 election campaign, Stanfield ran on a platform of wage and price controls. Trudeau—in true style—mocked Stanfield for trying to say "Zap, you're frozen!" to the economy. Was it good policy? Apparently Trudeau felt so, for one year later, the newly re-elected Liberal prime minister would implement the very same controls proposed by Stanfield.

Nevertheless, at the height of the '74 campaign, Stanfield had reason to be optimistic—until the appearance of the now-infamous "fumble photo."

The fateful photograph was taken on May 30, 1974, during a cross-country tour to rally support for the Tories. As he waited for his plane to refuel in North Bay, Ontario, Stanfield and an aide decided to toss around the pigskin.

Doug Ball, a staff photographer with Canadian Press, took plenty of frames of Stanfield successfully catching the football on the tarmac. But it was the fumble that made front-page news the next day—appearing in the *Globe and Mail* accompanied by the headline: "A political fumble?"

The image of Stanfield "knock-kneed, hands-clasped, awkwardly grimacing," is the defining moment of the politician's otherwise successful career, says Ball. The photograph—and the ensuing fallout—changed the way the game of politics was played in Canada. With cameras rolling and photographers on standby, politicians had to watch more than their words. Image became a deciding factor at the ballot box.

Today, Stanfield is often called by his supporters the greatest prime minister Canada never had. Did this photograph directly lead to his defeat? Maybe not—but it was undoubtedly a contributing factor. It certainly ushered in a new era of image politics.

"I still get in fights with people who are upset with me for taking that photo," Ball says. "But Stanfield was a great guy with a good sense of humour, and he never cringed at it."

70

Robert Stanfield fumbles his football, May 30, 1974.

Henry Morgentaler, March 29, 1975.

71

Inspiration or Infuriation?

Abortion advocate polarized the nation

ANDRÉ PICARD

It says a lot about Henry Morgentaler that, on his way to prison, he is sporting a Cheshire cat grin and flashing a victory sign.

The day this photo was taken, March 27, 1975, he was only a few years into his four-decade-long battle to ensure safe, legal abortions, but he could already taste victory.

Morgentaler, a Polish immigrant to Canada, began practising medicine in 1950. In the 1950s and 1960s, abortion and birth control were illegal in Canada, but many physicians provided these services on the sly. That all changed in 1967 when Morgentaler testified at a parliamentary committee and demanded that women be given the right to safe abortion. Soon after, he put his words into action, openly performing abortions in his private Montreal clinic, and virtually daring the authorities to charge him.

At the time, a pregnancy could be terminated only if it put a woman's life in danger. But the women's rights movement was burgeoning and there was pressure to liberalize the law. In 1969, the Criminal Code was amended to allow abortion if a hospital's therapeutic abortion committee gave its okay. However, under those rules, Morgentaler's practice remained illegal, and in 1970 he was charged—beginning what would become a lengthy legal battle.

A jury acquitted him of performing an illegal abortion, but the Quebec Court of Appeal overturned the ruling; Morgentaler remains the only Canadian ever jailed after being acquitted by a jury of his peers. A second trial saw him cleared again, but Morgentaler ended up serving a total of ten months in prison, suffering a heart attack while in solitary confinement. A first challenge of the law to the Supreme Court of Canada was unsuccessful; but in 1988, the country's highest court ruled that Canada's abortion law was unconstitutional.

The doctor's high public profile made him a lightning rod for criticism—and much more. His Toronto clinic was bombed, and Morgentaler lived much of his adult life with death threats hanging over his head.

A key figure in the moral, ethical, and political debates surrounding women's reproductive rights, Morgentaler drifted from the public eye for a number of years. He stopped personally performing abortions in 2006 due to heart-related problems, but he continued to operate six private clinics. His legal battles also continued, mostly related to the lack of access to abortion in less populous parts of Canada.

In recent years, he has received many accolades—and that has rekindled the abortion debate. In 2005, the University of Western Ontario granted him an honorary law degree, sparking protests and counter-protests. Then, on Canada Day 2008, he received the Order of Canada amid controversy. In a brief acceptance speech, Morgentaler said: "Canada's one of the few places in the world where freedom of speech and choice prevail in a truly democratic fashion."

Whether this photo inspires or infuriates you, there's no question that Henry Morgentaler has left an indelible mark on Canada's health and legal systems.

An Olympian Effort

Montreal Games scored with Canadians

RICHARD W. POUND

July 17, 1976, the date of the opening ceremony of the Olympic Games in Montreal, was a day that many feared might never come. Yet, for those struggling to get the facilities ready on time, the day seemed to arrive all too soon.

These were the first Olympic Games to be awarded to a Canadian city, a campaign won by the charismatic mayor of Montreal, Jean Drapeau, who managed in the process to beat out the world's superpowers, the United States and the U.S.S.R.

Many factors combined to add to the normal challenges of staging the Olympic Games. Financing arrangements had not been confirmed between the various levels of government, and contracts had not been negotiated with organized labour. Meanwhile, resentment simmered in the rest of the country over Montreal's hosting both Expo 67 and the Olympics. Throw into the mix unprecedented worldwide inflation, an absurdly expensive stadium design, the massacre at the Munich Games in 1972, and the need for the Quebec government to step in to take over the construction projects, and the result was uncertainty, bordering on despair, regarding the eventual outcome.

Public perceptions regarding the costs of the Games were exacerbated by Drapeau's resolute refusal to separate the Olympic-related costs from the main infrastructure budget.

Many questions lingered as the Games neared. What reception would greet Queen Elizabeth—whose 1964 visit to Quebec had been marred with violent protests—as the province moved inexorably toward a *séparatiste* government (elected within four months after the Games)? How would Drapeau be received by his fellow citizens?

And then there were the political emergencies—controversies over the participation of Taiwan, as well as the boycott of several African and West Indian teams—which were mishandled by the International Olympic Committee in the final few days before the Games began.

But on the big day, the opening ceremony was spectacular. Spectators were awed by the stadium. The crowd was polite in its reception of the Queen, enthusiastic—despite the cost overruns—in its support of the mayor, and captivated by the music of André Mathieu (the best music ever played, still to this date, at an Olympic opening ceremony). And the crowd was moved by the human touch of using two young athletes, Sandra Henderson and Stéphane Préfontaine, to light the Olympic flame in the stadium.

The Games were a huge success and security, raised to a new level following Munich, was discreet and effective. Conditions for the athletes, including competition venues and a magnificent Olympic Village, were superb, as was the organization of the events. This, despite the domestic issue of costs, was the beginning of a well-deserved reputation for Canada throughout the world as a first-class Olympic host.

Alas, Canada failed to win a single gold medal—and remains the only host country for a Summer Olympics to hold that distinction.

Opening ceremonies of the Montreal Summer Olympics, 1976.

Margaret Trudeau at Studio 54, May 23, 1979.

The "Bye-Bye Boogie"

Infamous two-step titillated the tabloids

PAUL JONES

Where have we heard this story before?

Aloof bachelor of regal mien marries vivacious ingénue much his junior. She bears his photogenic sons but chafes at protocol and resents his emotional distance. Her increasingly erratic behaviour places her firmly in the media spotlight, amplifying her every misstep. Soon, she leaves hubby amidst cover-story hoopla in *People* and whispers of liaisons with unsuitable men.

As later with Princess Diana, so too for Margaret Trudeau in the 1970s: our own made-in-Canada Cinderella-story-gone-sour—sans the tragic ending.

In the spring of 1979, Canadians were engrossed in the closest election campaign since Pierre Trudeau's win in 1968. At the time separated from the prime minister for two years, Margaret Trudeau had dabbled in film and was a semi-regular in jet-set circles. She had just published her confessional memoir, *Beyond Reason*, to taunts of "trash" and "gossip." A *Globe and Mail* columnist had branded her "the first lady of scandal."

In April, as the campaign raged, Margaret returned to New York to promote her book. She often turned up at the infamous Studio 54, and these outings were faithfully reported in Canadian media alongside mid-campaign denials of an affair with Ted Kennedy. The universal impression was of Maggie fiddling while Pierre surely burned.

Such antics did not conform to business as usual for the wife of a prime minister—a position so low-key we haven't even come up with a snappier term for it. And no wonder—for twenty-seven years (1921 to 1948), bachelors had served as PM for all but five months. Three successive wives of prime ministers—Jeanne Saint-Laurent, Olive Diefenbaker, and Maryon Pearson—had largely avoided the spotlight. Margaret Trudeau was different. The camera loved her—and she reciprocated the affection.

The wee hours of May 23, 1979, were a case in point. At 12:46 a.m., Pierre Trudeau had conceded defeat to Joe Clark. Yet here was Margaret Trudeau apparently celebrating—dancing frenetically in disco pants and impossible stilettos. To a reporter present at Studio 54 she spoke positively about her husband. But trust Fleet Street to cut to the chase: "Bye-Bye Boogie! Margaret Dances on as Trudeau Gets the Boot," blared *The Sun*.

Viewed through the lens of decades of increasingly cheesy tabloid journalism (think: Britney Spears, Paris Hilton, and *Girls Gone Wild*), Maggie's dancing seems pretty small beer. But we were new then to celebrity culture—*People* had been founded just five years earlier and most of its rivals were still to come. Not surprisingly perhaps, columnists and ordinary Canadians found Margaret's actions shocking. Thirty years on, one is struck by the condescension, vitriol, and outright misogyny that characterized their comments.

Would they have spoken differently if they knew Margaret Trudeau had a recognized psychiatric condition? Now past sixty, she has been diagnosed with bipolar disorder and has become an advocate on behalf of those similarly afflicted. Perhaps her finest fifteen minutes are yet to come.

A Final Farewell

Last ride for a Western hero

DEBORAH GREY

It was the least we could do. Yet for many of us, it was also the most we could do.

There was no way during harvest we could get away to Saskatoon for his funeral. Besides, the place would be packed out.

John Diefenbaker was a legend in the West. With thousands expected to attend the memorial event, there would be no room for everyone at the service. But this seemed better, in a way. Average folks could pay their own respects, in their own fields, as Diefenbaker's funeral train slowly made its way across the Prairies. Many Westerners would remember that scene for the rest of their lives.

John George Diefenbaker was just a month shy of his eighty-fourth birthday when he died on August 16, 1979. He was predeceased by his wife, Olive, who died in 1976. Considered Parliament Hill's elder statesman, the former prime minister was famous for his thunderous oratory and sharp wit. He also never forgot where he came from; he was a Westerner through and through.

Diefenbaker planned his own funeral train procession, which began in Ottawa and made two two-hour-long stops—in Winnipeg and in Prince Albert, Saskatchewan—as it travelled westward toward Saskatoon. As the Via Rail train passed through golden fields of wheat and barley, average Canadians lined the tracks. Diefenbaker was coming home, and for many, it was like having their own private audience with the man who had been their leader.

For many Westerners—especially the many immigrants who made the Prairies their new home—Diefenbaker was their champion. Fresh from the old country, some immigrants felt the stigma of not being considered "fully" Canadian. Diefenbaker changed all that. He insisted that every one of us was simply a Canadian—"no hyphens, no explanations." His words lifted the spirits of all those who came to Canada to start a new life.

Farming is a tough lifestyle to choose. Homesteaders plant their crops, keep an eye to the weather, and hope for the best. What a great day it was when Diefenbaker managed to open China's markets up to our wheat crops! He stabilized commodity prices and made many Western farmers finally feel like they were an important part of the nation's economy. He was a leader, that man.

How fitting it was that he was coming home at the height of the harvest. As the funeral train neared, we waited for the sound of that mournful whistle, the one that we would remember forever. Soon, children were shouting: "Here it comes. I hear the horn! I see the smoke!" As it drew closer, we all grew quiet; we knew something powerful was happening.

The train slowed as it passed by. The mood was sombre. This was the last ride for a Canadian hero and we had a front-row seat. With hats off, we bade farewell to The Chief. It was the least we could do; it was the most we could do.

74

John Diefenbaker's funeral train, near Saskatoon, August 21, 1979.

PART FOUR

FUTURE FOCUS
1980–PRESENT

F or almost 113 years, Canada had defied the odds. We were an illogical country, created almost in spite of ourselves, too rugged and too large to tame, too cold to settle, divided by language and religion. Famously dismissed in the eighteenth century as nothing more than a "few acres of snow," Canada would later be described as "two nations warring in the bosom of a single state"—not exactly the recipe for a trouble-free future.

And yet, somehow we not only survived, we thrived.

By 1980 though, it looked as if the odds had finally caught up with us. It was the end of May and Canadians everywhere anxiously awaited the results of a referendum in Quebec. The question on the ballot spoke of something called "sovereignty-association," but everyone knew what was really at stake—separation, a new Quebec nation, and the end of Canada as we knew it. Ultimately, Quebecers chose Canada; all Canadians awoke the next day exhausted from the country's near-death experience.

Amid the post-referendum gloom was a spark of hope. It came in the form of a young man who, after dipping his artificial leg in the cold Atlantic, set out to cross the country to raise awareness of cancer.

The eighties saw us finally freed of the colonial ties that had bound Canada to Britain. At the same time, we sought closer economic ties with America—making a political and socio-economic shift that left many Canadians increasingly uncomfortable.

In the 1990s, centuries-old divisions between English and French, and aboriginals and non-aboriginals, flared anew. Suddenly, the dreaded C-word—*Constitution*—was making headlines again. For women, it was a decade to celebrate new achievements, such as the first female prime minister, and the first Canadian woman in space, even as we mourned the victims of a massacre in Montreal in 1989 that continues to haunt us today.

As we say farewell to film photography and enter the digital age, someone taking a snapshot of Canada in the early years of the twenty-first century might find plenty of cause for concern. Faced with climate change, a global economic downturn, and engaged in a war in Afghanistan, it's tough to see the right way forward. And yet, when we picture just how far we've come in four centuries—from a small colony huddled on the banks of the St. Lawrence, to a modern, multicultural nation 33-million-Canadians strong, that embraces its diversity—there's reason for hope.

Throughout our history, we have repelled invasions, endured disasters, and carved cities from forests, mountains and prairies. The story of Canada is the story of survival. The future lies before us like an undeveloped photo, awaiting revelation.

—Mark Reid

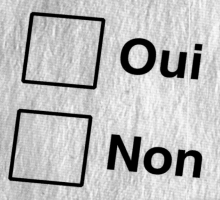

Oui

Non

75

Quebec premier René Lévesque is overcome
with emotion after losing the 1980 referendum.

Until Next Time!

Separation anxiety followed referendum loss

JACQUES LACOURSIÈRE

"If I understand you well, you are telling me: 'Until next time!' In the meantime, and with the same composure displayed throughout the campaign, we will have to put this one aside this time. It is not easy. It is difficult. It is more painful than any electoral defeat. And I know what I'm talking about. . . ."

It was with these words that Quebec Premier René Lévesque, leader of the separatist Parti Québécois, addressed the nine thousand supporters who had gathered at Montreal's Paul Sauvé Arena, on May 20, 1980—the night of the first Quebec referendum.

Lévesque had likely dreamed of this moment—of stepping up to the microphone to announce that Quebecers had finally voted to become a nation. However, when the ballots were finally counted, it was clear the dream was but a fleeting thing. The No side had captured 59.5 percent of the vote, with 85 percent of registered voters exercising their right at the ballot box. Quebec would remain a part of Canada.

Things had started to unravel six days earlier, on May 14, when Prime Minister Pierre Trudeau launched into the fray. Until then, the No campaign had been largely a provincially run affair, headed by Claude Ryan, leader of Quebec's Liberal Party.

Standing in Paul Sauvé Arena, Trudeau promised that if the No side won, he would reform the Canadian Constitution to address the concerns of Quebecers. "We are willing to lay our seats in the House on the line for change," he added. "We will not stop until we have done that."

Lévesque responded angrily: "For Quebecers, Trudeau embodies who they would have to be. And me, who they are."

Lévesque's cause had not been helped by the overly convoluted ballot question that spoke not of outright separation, but of something called sovereignty-association with Canada. Trudeau, sensing an opportunity, said Canada would refuse a sovereignty-association with Quebec, filling many Quebecers with uncertainty as they headed to the ballot box.

Lévesque would be forever scarred by the results of the first referendum. In 1982, he refused to join the other provinces in supporting the patriation of the Constitution. However, in 1984, he decided to take a *beau risque* and support Brian Mulroney—an anglophone Quebecer—for prime minister. Lévesque hoped Mulroney was right when he said he wanted to invite Quebec to "re-enter the ranks of Canadians with honour and dignity."

It was too much for hardline separatists in the Parti Québécois. In 1985, Lévesque stepped down both as premier and as leader of the PQ. This marked the end of his political career.

Lévesque died two years later, in 1987. The party he founded, the PQ, remains a force in Quebec politics. His statue now stands outside Quebec's Parliament building—and in an ironic twist, it stands . . . on *federal* land.

Terry's Journey

A story in shadow and light

CHRIS WEBB

Terry Fox believed in miracles. He said he had no other choice.

In this evocative photograph, Terry is silhouetted by the headlights of a police cruiser rolling behind him on an early summer morning in 1980. The image instantly evokes the memories that many Canadians still hold dear of Terry during his Marathon of Hope, as well as the unwavering determination he showed during those inspiring months.

Why does Terry's journey from the cancer ward to the open road still evoke such emotion among Canadians? The answer lies in the story of Terry's life and, sadly, the circumstances surrounding his death.

Terry was always the athletic type and hoped someday to become a gym teacher. He was just eighteen when he lost his right leg to a rare form of cancer. The experience of being in a hospital with other cancer patients moved him so deeply that he devoted the rest of his life to fighting the disease. Three years after the amputation, he decided he'd run across Canada to raise money for cancer research.

His Marathon of Hope began April 12, 1980, in St. John's, Newfoundland, and ended five months later on the outskirts of Thunder Bay, Ontario. The cancer had spread to his lungs and forced him to abandon the cross-Canada run.

Throughout Terry's journey, Canadians had marvelled at his sheer courage and determination. That grit comes through in this image. With his left leg suspended in the air, the young man leans on his prosthetic leg in that characteristic gait that can belong only to Terry. Some photos go beyond capturing the moment; some capture the soul of the subject. This is one of them.

The photographer who took the picture, Peter Martin, remembers well the morning he took it. He woke up early, eager to get the jump on the other photojournalists who would be waiting on the highway just outside of Oakville, Ontario. It had rained the night before and the wet asphalt reflected the light of passing cars. Martin remembers capturing the photo, but had no idea it would portray Terry's persona so vividly.

Martin calls Terry a "pure heart" and fondly remembers spending the day with him and his brother, Darrell along the Trans-Canada Highway. "Terry just wanted ordinary Canadians to fight cancer by giving what they could," he says.

Since his death, the annual Terry Fox Run has collected more than $400 million for cancer research.

Whether or not Terry would have liked it, he has become a symbol for those struggling with disease and adversity. This photo captures that struggle: While bathing him in a halo of light, it leaves a dark shadow before him, one he would face on the road to Thunder Bay. He died on June 28, 1981, at the age of twenty-two.

76

30
Canada

I'm Supporting TERRY FOX

Terry Fox during his Marathon of Hope, July 13, 1980.

Bob and Doug McKenzie, ca. 1980–81.

77

Canuck Comedy Takes Off

Beer-drinking hosers made Canadian clichés cool

PAUL JONES

Toque-wearing, back bacon–frying, beer-guzzling (never in a glass, always directly from the stubby), Bob and Doug McKenzie beckoned us to the "Great White North," an alternate Canada unfrequented by us urban Canadians —and maybe, we suspected, entirely imaginary.

Yet we couldn't be sure. The locals in cottage country often seemed Bob and Doug-like (although their elders more closely resembled Don Harron's Charlie Farquharson). And who was the heartland market for Tim Hortons and the audience for Stompin' Tom, if not the McKenzie brothers and their ilk?

Anyway, it didn't much matter if they were realistic. They were funny—whether scheming to chisel free beer from the big breweries; or rolling their own smokes while wearing mittens; or singing a deliriously moronic version of "The Twelve Days of Christmas"; but mostly doing absolutely nada, long before *Seinfeld* became the TV show about nothing.

It almost didn't happen. Bob and Doug were not part of the first two seasons of *SCTV*. When the show moved from Global to CBC in 1980, the brass demanded more Canadian content. This seemed ridiculous to the overwhelmingly Canadian cast and crew. So, as a "mean-spirited joke" on their corporate masters, Rick Moranis (Bob) and Dave Thomas (Doug) conceived a two-minute segment incorporating every tired Canadian cliché that would fit. Lumberjack shirts. Parkas. Snowshoes. Hockey. A Mountie bust. And the "Koo-LOO-koo-koo-koo-koo-koo-KOOOOO theme, " an impressionistic composite of the recorder sound tracks seemingly omnipresent on Canadian nature documentaries of the era.

To everyone's amazement, these sketches were an immense hit, not just in Canada but also the United States (although we suspected Americans were laughing at us, not with us). Soon "hoser," "take off!" and "beauty" entered our vernacular (and, later, the lexicon). We added "eh" to the end of every sentence as a mark of our ironic pseudo-unsophistication. Canadian corn was the new cool.

An album followed in 1981, with Rush's Geddy Lee providing the vocal on the Top 20 hit "Take Off!" Then came the 1983 movie, *Strange Brew*, featuring Max von Sydow—yes, *that* Max von Sydow—as a demented brewmaster. Even decades later, in 2007, CBC was airing the aptly titled *Two-Four Anniversary* special, hosted entirely deadpan by former prime minister Paul Martin.

Just as Charlie Farquharson had foreshadowed Bob and Doug, they prefigured Red Green and his doofus nephew, Harold, and in more baleful recent times, Ricky, Julian, and Bubbles of *Trailer Park Boys*. Would we have so keenly welcomed Joe and his "I am Canadian" rant from that beer commercial if the gentler Bob and Doug had not prepared the way?

Notwithstanding their constant bickering and petty scheming, Bob and Doug were decent guys—"nice," in a word. The world always needs more of that, Canadian cliché or not. And if you don't agree, you're a total hosehead.

Signing Off

Patriated Constitution signalled era of independence

MICHAEL BLISS

Signing ceremonies are usually calm and happy events. A pen moves across a paper, a few hands clap, there are smiles.

Like tombstones, photos of signing events capture the peace and serenity at the end of the story. Queen Elizabeth II seems entirely content to be formally surrendering all British involvement in the Constitution of Canada. Prime Minister Pierre Trudeau is positively happy as he brings to an end more than two centuries of British lawmaking in this part of the world. R.I.P. Wolfe, and Montcalm, and 1763. R.I.P. foreign rule in Canada. Britain signs off.

Canada's march to full formal independence had been long and mercifully peaceful. Some serious impediments had remained after the 1931 Statute of Westminster seemed to grant full self-government to Britain's former "dominions." Canada's written constitution, the British North America Act, was still legislation by the Parliament of Great Britain, and could be amended only by that body.

If the Canadians could ever get their act together and agree on a proposal for an all-Canadian Constitution—the problem was disagreement between the two levels of government, national and provincial, in the Canadian federation—the British would have been happy to wash their hands completely of Canadian affairs. In 1982, the Canadian Constitution was finally brought home, finally patriated.

Along the way there had been tears, conflict, and, at the end, casualties. In its determination to break the jurisdictional impasse on the Constitution, the Trudeau government had pressured recalcitrant provinces with the threat of unilateral action, had bent to their resistance by compromising the effectiveness of the new Charter of Rights and Freedoms it was inserting in the Constitution and, finally, had proceeded against the wishes of the government of Quebec, led at the time by the separatist premier, René Lévesque.

As Queen Elizabeth signs the Canada Act in Ottawa, no provincial premiers are in the picture, only federal civil servants. The weather that April 17 was cloudy, and immediately after the signing ceremony the skies turned stormy, both literally and politically. Canadians fought for another decade about packages of amendments to the Constitution, mostly designed to mollify Quebec. Neither the Meech Lake nor the Charlottetown constitutional accords received legislative sanction, however, and Quebec still pronounces itself estranged from the Canadian constitutional family.

It's a family feud, however, a quarrel among offspring. With this photo the mother country leaves it up to the Canadian children to run their own affairs, for weal or woe.

78

Prime Minister Pierre Trudeau and Queen Elizabeth sign the Constitution in Ottawa, April 17, 1982.

Canadian Astronauts Ken Money and Roberta Bondar get a feel for zero gravity during training on board NASA's KC135 aircraft on Dec. 18, 1984.

79

Star-Struck Scientist

First female astronaut inspired a generation

MARK REID

Even as a young girl, Roberta Bondar seemed destined to reach for the stars.

Growing up along the shores of Lake Superior, she spent countless nighttime hours gazing at the brilliant celestial canopy. Sometimes she'd catch sight of a satellite coursing on its silent orbit. Caught up with wonder, she would suddenly picture herself soaring along with it.

"I had a vision of going into space," says the Sault Ste. Marie–born physician, scientist, astronaut, and photographer.

For a girl from Northern Ontario, becoming an astronaut likely seemed an out-of-this-world ambition. Luckily, her supportive family fuelled her dream. An aunt who worked at the Kennedy Space Center would send her NASA space mission patches. An uncle gave her a microscope and a crystal radio kit. And at eight and a half—an age at which many girls were still dallying with dolls—she was building plastic rockets, and then shooting black-and-white stills of them with her Eastman camera.

It would be this combination of passions—a love of space and of photography—that helped propel Bondar into the history books in 1992 as Canada's first female astronaut in space.

Bondar was not the first Canadian in space; that honour goes to astronaut Marc Garneau. Yet while Garneau inspired all Canadians with his achievement, it can be argued that Bondar's impact, particularly on young women, had a deeper resonance. To them, Bondar was living proof that science wasn't just a man's game, that women could stand—or in the case of this photograph, float—as equals to their male counterparts.

Bondar spent eight days aboard the space shuttle *Discovery*, circling the globe 129 times. Among her many duties, she was assigned to shoot photographs of the Earth. Aiming her camera through a porthole, she shot up to 5,000 images in an eight-hour period. The experience— seeing the world as a fragile, swirling ball of greens, whites, and blues amid the blackness of space—was life-changing.

She returned to earth with a new mission—to share her passion for the planet with others.

"It would be great if everyone could go into space and see [that] this is all we have," she once said. "The things we are fighting over . . . are not that important compared to the continuation of life on the planet."

In the ensuing years, Bondar has published several books and earned many accolades. Named one of North America's greatest explorers by *Time* magazine, she has also received at least twenty-four honorary doctorates and is a member of the Order of Canada. Most importantly, Bondar reminds us all to seek out—and cherish—the beauty that surrounds us in the heavens and here on earth.

Call to Action

Musical supergroup made Canadians take note

DEBORAH MORRISON

The story of how Northern Lights—the Canadian supergroup that recorded "Tears Are Not Enough"—came together is legendary.

Canadian record producer David Foster took a call from American music impresario Quincy Jones shortly before lunch on Tuesday, February 5, 1985. Jones planned to produce an American follow-up to Bob Geldof's Band Aid recording of "Do They Know It's Christmas?" Jones wanted Foster to organize a Canadian contribution to include on the LP—but the recording had to be completed and delivered within a week.

Jim Vallance, the project's co-producer, explains: "We wrote the song on February 6 and 7, and we recorded it on Sunday, February 10. . . . It was essentially completed in five days. It was a near-impossible task getting all those people together on such short notice. Only someone like [talent agent] Bruce Allen could have pulled that off."

Indeed. Within five days Allen had recruited forty-four Canadian singers from every genre of the industry. This image unfolds like a who's who of the Canadian music industry. It must have been a groupie's dream outside Manta Sound Studios in Toronto that morning as legends such as Neil Young, Liona Boyd, Bryan Adams, Carol Baker, Oscar Peterson, Salome Bey, and even John Candy arrived. Most stayed true to character—Gordon Lightfoot opted for his old pickup truck, instead of a limo, for his ride. Joni Mitchell took a taxi. (No one recalls if it was big or yellow.)

The lyrics were as urgent as they were optimistic: "If we can pull together, / We could change the world forever. / Heaven knows that tears are not enough."

It was a powerful call to action, and Canadians answered, driving more than $3 million in record sales and charitable contributions to Ethiopian Famine Relief. Later that summer, Bob Geldof organized Live Aid, the first truly international charity concert. Within six months, this musical force changed the world's knowledge and attitude toward the growing crisis in Africa.

In the ensuing years, charity bands would come together and fall away for various causes. However, none would have the same power and impact in Canada as Northern Lights. Today, many believe that such a global convergence is likely never to repeat. "Now, twenty-five years and many benefits later, I think the music community is a bit jaded," Vallance says. "We tried to organize a Terry Fox benefit in 2007, and we couldn't get a single artist to commit. I mean, who could say no to Terry Fox?"

The cynical among us would say musicians are more notable these days for their clichéd excesses: sex, drugs, and bling. But that's not entirely true.

Some artists will always be activists, but the way they show their support is evolving. Canadian artists like Sarah McLachlan (Lilith Fair), Bruce Cockburn (Friends of the Earth), Sum 41 (War Child Canada), Chantal Kreviazuk (aboriginal youth), and many others contribute significantly to continuing efforts to change our world. The calls to action remain. It's up to us to answer.

Northern Lights records "Tears Are Not Enough" in Toronto on February 10, 1985.

80

81

The Mulroneys and Reagans singing "Irish Eyes Are Smiling," Quebec City, March 17, 1985.

The Shamrock Summit

Irish ballad hit sour political note

JACQUES POITRAS

The great free trade debate of 1988 may have had its start three years earlier, at the very moment this photograph was taken.

In March 1985, Prime Minister Brian Mulroney took a major step in his effort to improve Canada's relationship with the United States: He welcomed President Ronald Reagan to a lavish meeting in Quebec City. It was dubbed the "Shamrock Summit," because of the pair's Irish roots and because it fell on St. Patrick's Day. Mulroney would stress in his memoirs the substantial work accomplished, including a joint declaration directing officials to look at the eventual lowering of trade barriers.

Canadians, however, would remember the moment during a gala concert when Mulroney, Reagan and their wives, Mila Mulroney and Nancy Reagan, were invited onstage by singer Maureen Forrester to join her in singing "When Irish Eyes Are Smiling." Standing hand-in-hand, with green streamers falling around them, the eager quartet belted out the ballad: "When Irish hearts are happy, / All the world seems bright and gay."

Unfortunately for Mulroney, not everyone was charmed by the performance. The former prime minister would recall: "Canadians in general loved the Irish duet, but the CBC replayed the clip constantly with commentary that it was symbolic of a humiliating example of 'toadyism' and a subordination of Canada's interests."

As the free trade debate unfolded, the scene lurked in the psyches of Canadians leery of closer ties to the United States. Perhaps the image merged with an anecdote from Mulroney's childhood, when, back home in Baie Comeau, Quebec, he had sung at the request of Colonel Robert R. McCormick, the American owner of the town's mill and its "absentee feudal lord," as one biographer put it.

When we collectively searched our souls for how we felt about a sweeping trade treaty with the United States, we thought back to the Shamrock Summit and that look in Mulroney's eyes: Was he too anxious to please the Americans? Did he, in his need for approval, give away too much? The opponents of the agreement certainly exploited that sentiment.

Speaking to Peter C. Newman in 1994, Mulroney predicted, "Twenty-five years from now there's going to be the biggest goddamned banquet you ever saw to celebrate the Free Trade Agreement, but I'm not going to be able to get into the room because [union leader] Bob White and [activist] Judy Rebick are going to be chairing it and saying it was their idea. That's the way history works."

Well, not quite. It has been two decades now since the great debate, and feelings about Mulroney and his agreement have diverged. The left is still not onside, but there is a rough consensus in the broad centre of the Canadian political spectrum that free trade was a good idea.

The former prime minister himself still bristles, as evidenced by his periodic attempts to defend his tenure, including that iconic moment in Quebec City in 1985. We might measure how he has fared by asking whether any subsequent Canadian prime minister would ever allow himself to be so photographed.

White Wolf

Future uncertain for Arctic's inhabitants

KEN McGOOGAN

"As much as it touches a feared aspect in us," Jim Brandenburg says, "the wolf is a symbol of wildness" with which we are striving to reconcile. In this picture, which the acclaimed wildlife photographer took on Ellesmere Island in 1987, a white wolf bounds across ice floes high above the Arctic Circle.

Brandenburg had discovered a pack of wolves that showed no fear of humans, probably because they had had little or no contact with us. The photographer has captured a fleeting instant when the dominant male of the pack bounds from one floe to the next, hunting waterfowl. Under a rocky outcrop on the nearby beach, Brandenburg tells us, the wolf had left behind six ravenous cubs.

In 1989, *National Geographic* magazine named this image, "White Wolf," one of the 100 best photographs of all time—recognizing, obviously, that it resonates far beyond this frozen moment. The glorious, elemental backdrop—ice, water, sky, and scudding clouds—is one of the most precarious on earth.

Ellesmere Island, the tenth-largest island in the world, forms part of Nunavut. It includes Cape Columbia, the most northerly point in Canada, and its largest community, Grise Fjord, is home to about 150 Inuit.

Ellesmere is adjacent to Greenland, which lies directly across Kane Basin and Kennedy Channel, which narrows to a width of thirty kilometres. Like Greenland, much of Ellesmere is covered with ice and glaciers. As late as the nineteenth century, a massive ice shelf ran unbroken along the northwest coast for 500 kilometres.

During the twentieth century, as a result of global warming, great chunks of thick, landfast sea ice broke off and floated away to melt. The original ice shelf became five separate ice shelves—but these, too, have begun breaking off. In September 2008, the 4,500-year-old Markham Ice Shelf broke off and drifted into the Arctic Ocean, turning fifty square kilometres of landfast ice into fast-melting sea ice.

This might sound innocuous. But such changes transform the habitat for algae, invertebrates, and waterfowl—the very waterfowl on which the Arctic wolf feeds. A recent scientific study showed that warming and evaporation have altered the chemistry of the ponds and wetlands where the wolves hunt. Researchers needed hip waders to reach the ponds in the 1980s, but by 2006, the same areas were dry enough to burn.

The white wolf, that most evocative symbol of the northern wild, has a lifespan of eighteen years. The graceful, leaping creature captured by Brandenburg lives no more. But what of the six cubs the wolf left on the beach? And what of their offspring?

This photo makes us wonder if the northern wild has a future.

82

Lone white wolf, Ellesmere Island, 1987.

Wayne Gretzky announces his trade to the L.A. Kings during a press conference in Edmonton, August 9, 1988.

83

The Trade

Sale of the Great One sent shockwaves through NHL

PAUL JONES

The Great One had rarely been greater.

In 1988, Wayne Gretzky led his Edmonton Oilers to their fourth Stanley Cup in five years. He set playoff scoring records that still stand, scored the winning goal in the clinching game and was named the playoffs' MVP. In a serendipitous moment, he gathered his celebrating teammates for an on-ice photo with Lord Stanley's mug, inaugurating what is now a time-honoured tradition.

Yet just weeks later, on August 9, "Number 99" tearfully announced at a press conference in Edmonton that he had requested a trade to the Los Angeles Kings in order to be close to his new wife, aspiring actress Janet Jones, who was expecting a baby.

From the start, opinion was divided—and heated. Did he jump, or was he pushed? If pushed, by whom? If he jumped, why? Was it a good deal for the Oilers? For the Kings? For Gretzky himself? How would Edmonton survive the loss of its most high-profile ambassador? What did this mean for hockey in the United States—and in Canada?

Everyone had an opinion. Some thought Gretzky needed new challenges, others pointed to Canada's high taxes. Many Oilers fans blamed Janet, seeing her as Yoko Ono to Gretzky's Lennon. The NDP, in vintage flat-earth mode, demanded that the federal government cancel the trade. Former Oilers star Paul Coffey, who had been traded in 1987 for financial reasons, charged that Gretzky had been treated as "just a piece of meat." Clearly Peter Pocklington, the owner of the Oilers, needed the $15 million that came with the deal.

From all accounts, Gretzky was a stand-up guy who hated to leave the fans and his team-mates, but the outpouring of emotion at the press conference seemed to go way beyond that. Maybe his legendary sixth sense, so useful on the ice, told him that the glory days were over. Only twenty-seven at the time of the trade, he would never again hoist the Stanley Cup in his eleven remaining seasons.

Or maybe Gretzky had a moment of clarity about his business associates. Has any sports figure been as ill-starred in his team owners? (Consider the Oilers' Nelson Skalbania and Peter Pocklington, or the Kings' Bruce McNall: collapsed ventures, bankruptcies, court judgments.)

Most dismaying for Canadians, Wayne Gretzky—our Captain Canada—has turned out to be the single most powerful tool utilized by the NHL in its ill-fated mission to bring hockey to the U.S. Sunbelt, at the expense of hockey in Canada. Soon after Gretzky's arrival in L.A., the NHL added two more California teams (Anaheim and San Jose). Meanwhile, Canada lost two teams—the Quebec Nordiques (now the Colorado Avalanche) and the Winnipeg Jets (now the Phoenix Coyotes, co-owned and coached by Gretzky himself). There are now half again as many teams in Sunbelt states as in all of Canada. As to Janet, a home base in L.A. was clearly over-rated: she's had exactly seven TV, film, and video acting credits since 1988. Gretzky's Coyotes, meanwhile, skate on thin financial ice.

None of it worked out for anyone. The fans were right: Gretzky should have toughed it out in Edmonton. No wonder he wept.

Tarnished Gold

Sprinter went from hero to villain in record time

RICHARD W. POUND

For about one month every four years, Canada retreats from its only universally recognized religion—ice hockey—to focus on the Summer Olympic Games and to wonder, in the aftermath, why Canadians do not do better. The year 1988 was no exception, although there were high hopes for a young Canadian sprinter in the 100 metres—the signature event of the Olympic Games.

His name was Ben Johnson, a Jamaican-born Torontonian. In 1984, he had finished third in the Los Angeles Games behind the American superstar Carl Lewis, the 1983 world champion. Johnson's surprising success had offered a glimmer of hope for the future.

By 1988, it had been sixty years since a Canadian—Percy Williams at the 1928 Amsterdam Games—had won the sprint. Could Ben Johnson reverse the trend?

Coached by Charlie Francis out of the Mazda track club in Toronto, Johnson continued to improve, eventually emerging as Lewis's chief rival. The two athletes were almost perfect foils for each other: Lewis was tall, handsome, and articulate, with a slow start and a powerful finish; Johnson was short, plain, hesitant of speech and manner, with a blazing start, but a less spectacular finishing kick. Johnson served notice on Lewis that Seoul would be a showdown when he trounced the American at the 1987 world championships in Rome. A year later, tensions in Seoul were particularly high and feelings between the two athletes well short of fraternal.

The start of the final was clean and, as expected, Johnson exploded into an early lead. By sixty metres into the race, however, Johnson was surrendering nothing to Lewis's fabled finishing speed. If anything, his lead increased, enough that well before the end of the race—as shown in the photograph—he could afford to look over at Lewis and disdainfully raise his hand in victory.

Johnson charged across the finish line to set a remarkable new world record of 9.79 seconds. It was a defining moment for the Canadian—whose margin of victory over his hated rival was unprecedented—and for Canada, which basked in his reflected glory. David had dispatched the American Goliath.

Then disaster struck. Word came from the International Olympic Committee that Johnson had tested positive for stanozolol, a prohibited anabolic steroid. Stripped of his gold medal, he fled Seoul in disgrace. Only then did people begin to question how this could have happened.

The Canadian government soon established a commission of inquiry headed by Charles Dubin, former chief justice of Ontario. Evidence was provided that showed regular drug use by Canadian athletes. Sweeping changes were put in place within Canadian sport based on Dubin's report.

With the exception of Donovan Bailey in 1996, no Canadian has since won the Olympic 100 metres. Meanwhile, many athletes who have won—including finalists in Johnson's race in Seoul—have been exposed as drug cheats. Bailey's clean victory provided Canadians some feelings of redemption, but for many, Johnson's name remains synonymous with the ongoing fight against doping in sports.

Ben Johnson wins 100-metre gold at the 1988 Summer Olympics in Seoul, South Korea.

84

85

A police officer takes down decorations after the Polytechnique massacre in Montreal on December 6, 1989.

Horror and Heartbreak
Tragic rampage forced rethink of gun laws
DEBORAH MORRISON

On December 6, 1989, shortly before 5:00 p.m., twenty-five-year-old Marc Lépine walked into École Polytechnique in Montreal armed with a hunting rifle he had purchased just two weeks earlier from a local sporting goods store. Over the next twenty minutes he would traverse all three floors of the engineering building hunting down women. He killed fourteen women and wounded ten women and four men.

The rampage finally ended when Lépine took his own life.

Inside the school's cafeteria, waiting for the coroners and family members to arrive, a plain-clothes police officer had drawn the curtains and begun to remove the Christmas decorations that had suddenly lost all meaning. Behind him was a gruesome and heartbreaking scene—the body of one of the slain women, slumped over in a chair.

At precisely this moment, photojournalist Allen McInnis—aided by two students who boosted him up to an outside window—positioned his camera through an opening in the curtains and captured the horrible scene on film.

This disturbing photo is one of the most enduring images of the Montreal Massacre. It has also become one of the most analyzed and controversial published news images in Canadian history.

In Montreal, the *Gazette* ran the photo on its front page, outraging many readers. Phone lines soon lit up with more than 400 calls from readers who were angered by its graphic nature and its invasiveness. Another 100 written letters followed, echoing similar sentiments.

Without a doubt the photo captured the inexorable brutality and senselessness of Lépine's actions. But it did more than that. The image cast an unavoidable spotlight on the fact that this wasn't a completely random event—it was a deliberate act of violence against women. The event also forced Canadians to begin talking about uncomfortable issues of gender roles and gender equity.

There are likely no words, no deeds that can comfort the families of the fourteen women murdered on that stark December day. To them, Lépine is the thief who robbed them of a lifetime of future joys with their loved ones.

For the rest of us, we are still feeling the impacts of his mad actions.

In 1991, a now-annual National Day of Remembrance and Action on Violence Against Women was established to recognize the anniversary of the deaths. A companion White Ribbon Campaign—first organized by a group of Ontario activists that included *Corner Gas* star Eric Peterson and federal NDP Leader Jack Layton—has a now international mission to encourage more men and boys to speak out against all forms of violence against women.

The murders also precipitated a major change in our gun control laws. In 1990, Heidi Rathjen, a survivor from the shootings, joined with Wendy Cukier to form the Coalition for Gun Control. The group became a driving force behind the establishment of Canada's current gun control laws and the controversial gun registry.

Act of Defiance

Famous "no" vote sank Meech Lake Accord

WINONA WHEELER

The iconic image of Elijah Harper holding his eagle feather in the Manitoba Legislature symbolizes not only the death of the Meech Lake Accord in 1990, but also the growing strength of First Nations' unrest and clout in the Canadian political scene.

The Meech Lake Accord was a constitutional amendment package negotiated in 1987 to gain Quebec's acceptance of the Constitution Act of 1982. Among its provisions was the recognition of Quebec as a "distinct society" within Canada.

The provinces were each given a three-year deadline to ratify the controversial accord. On June 12, 1990—just eleven days before the June 23, 1990, ratification deadline—Manitoba Premier Gary Filmon asked MLAs to waive a two-day waiting period procedure that was required prior to the legislative debate. The waiver, considered a formality, required unanimous consent. When the vote was called, only one MLA, Elijah Harper, voted no.

"It is not easy for me to make this decision," Harper told the media afterwards, "but who is going to speak for us?" Harper, a member of the opposition NDP, was the only aboriginal MLA in Manitoba. Thanks to his no vote, public hearings into the Meech Lake Accord would have to be held before it could be voted on in the Legislature—with only nine days for the entire process.

As the drama unfolded, hundreds of First Nations people and their allies gathered outside the Legislative Assembly to show their support for Harper. Chanting "No to Meech Lake," they waved placards and beat traditional drums. Phil Fontaine—then serving as the Manitoba Regional Chief of the Assembly of First Nations—had masterminded the protest and had also identified the procedural provision that ultimately allowed Harper to block the legislative debate.

Fontaine and Harper stressed that while they did not oppose special status for Quebec, they were angry that special status for First Nations was not also recognized in the Meech Lake deal. According to Fontaine, of "particular concern was the big lie that Canada was made up of two founding nations, two official languages."

The Meech Lake Accord required unanimous consent from the provinces. When it became clear Manitoba would miss the ratification deadline, the federal government offered a three-month extension. A frustrated Newfoundland Premier Clyde Wells then decided to cancel the ratification vote in his province. The Meech Lake Accord was dead.

Harper, a reluctant hero from Red Sucker Lake in northern Manitoba, suddenly found himself in a media hailstorm. Voted "Newsmaker of the Year in Canada" by The Canadian Press, he was also named "Honorary Chief for Life" by his community.

The death of the Meech Lake Accord would have a profound impact. Several Quebec MPs would quit the Progressive Conservative and Liberal parties and help to form the separatist Bloc Québécois. In 1992, Canadians were asked in a referendum to support the Charlottetown Accord, another constitutional amendment package. It was defeated. And just over a year later, the federal P.C. government—which had initiated both the Meech Lake and Charlottetown Accords—would be decimated at the polls.

86

Manitoba NDP MLA Elijah Harper delays debate on Meech Lake Accord, June 19, 1990.

87

Kim Campbell poses with her barrister's robes, July 30, 1990

Naked Ambition

Politician's risqué pose earned her praise and pans

CHARLOTTE GRAY

A lawyer naked under her robes?! A candidate running bare-shouldered for the leadership of Canada?!

When this photograph was taken in 1990, Kim Campbell had just been made Canada's first female minister of justice in the Progressive Conservative government led by Brian Mulroney. B.C. photographer Barbara Woodley originally wanted the forty-three-year-old lawyer and Member of Parliament to pose with her cello, but Campbell had just picked up her new barrister's robes from the tailor. "Holding the robes while I was fully dressed would look silly," Campbell explains in her memoirs. Never one to avoid a risky step, she bared her shoulders. The photograph was exhibited in British Columbia without comment the same year.

Two years later, Mulroney's departure from office was imminent, and Campbell was increasingly mentioned as a potential successor. Everything about her was interpreted through the prism of her possible candidacy. In November 1992, an exhibition of Barbara Woodley's portraits of Canadian women was mounted at Ottawa's National Arts Centre, and the Campbell image caused a sensation. It was reproduced in the *Ottawa Citizen* under the caption "Doing Justice to Art," and an NDP MP compared Campbell to the singer Madonna, then in the coned-bra stage of her career. (Back then, the comparison was seen as unflattering; today, given Madonna's enduring celebrity, we're not so sure.) Within days, a British newspaper featured the picture with the caption "The Madonna of Canada," and the Italian press reported that Canada's minister of justice had posed with nude men. (A mistranslation, according to Campbell, of "bare shoulders.")

Campbell tried to defuse the issue by telling reporters that the difference between her and Madonna was the difference "between a strapless evening gown and a gownless evening strap." That quote got her even more publicity, and she was accused of deliberately raising her profile with the picture to further her political ambitions.

The rest of the story unfolded at warp speed. A few weeks later, Mulroney resigned. In June 1993, Campbell became Canada's first female prime minister. That fall, after Campbell had led the Progressive Conservative party for only five months, it was defeated resoundingly in a federal election and Campbell lost her own seat. She had run a lousy campaign, but victory was never really within her reach. The Mulroney regime had been deeply unpopular, and the Canadian electorate hungered for revenge. Campbell had been an impressive justice minister, but had no chance to demonstrate strength as a national leader.

Did this photograph help or hurt Campbell's career? It undoubtedly raised her profile, although it may have reinforced unfair suspicions that she was a lightweight. The image of a beautiful, brainy, and brave woman sandwiched between a sombre professional outfit and a pale gauzy background continues to intrigue observers.

One of those who admired it at the 1992 exhibit was former prime minister Pierre Trudeau. Campbell told him she posed this way because she had just picked up her robes. Trudeau paused, then mischievously asked, "And what were you doing before you picked them up?"

Standoff at Oka

Dramatic confrontation concerned all Canadians

CHRIS WEBB

It's an image that brings to mind a near civil war on Canadian soil.

A Canadian soldier and a Mohawk warrior—his face hidden by a camouflage balaclava—stare each other down amid the tall pines near Oka, Quebec.

Tempers are flaring. Negotiations have collapsed. The tension is razor-edged. This dramatic photograph captures the anger—and potential for violence—that epitomized the two-and-a-half-month standoff at the Kanesatake reserve near Oka in the summer of 1990. The image also served as a visual wake-up call for Canadians that First Nations would fight to protect what they felt was theirs.

For almost three centuries, the Mohawks had prevented development on land they considered to be their traditional burial grounds. When the town of Oka expropriated the area and proposed extending its nine-hole golf course to eighteen, the Mohawks barricaded the road to the reserve and declared the land to be their territory.

In July 1990—with the barricades still in place—more than 100 Sûreté du Québec officers came to Oka. They shot tear gas and exchanged gunshots with the demonstrators; after the smoke cleared, Corporal Marcel Lemay lay dead. The event marked a dramatic turning point in the conflict—and it wasn't over yet.

With Canadian troops on standby by August 8, a settlement brokered by Quebec's minister of native affairs collapsed. Soon, tanks were rolling in, and the prospect of further violence loomed.

The image of the baby-faced soldier, Patrick Cloutier, facing an armed, masked Brad Laroque appeared on front pages across the country, causing many to worry that the standoff would end in even more bloodshed.

Miraculously, it did not. On September 26, 1990, the final barricade came down and the Mohawks walked away from the burial site; thirty-four of them were arrested. Today, the Oka Golf Club remains a nine-hole course and the disputed land is now an extension of the Mohawk cemetery.

The standoff at Oka prompted the Standing Committee on Aboriginal Affairs to release a report that concluded: "Canadians want to see justice achieved for aboriginal people in Canada."

In the ensuing years, there have been other standoffs, at Ipperwash, Tyendinaga, and Grassy Narrows. This photo is a reminder to all Canadians that despite solid steps—such as the 2008 federal apology for residential schools and the creation of a native land claims commission—there is still work to be done to bridge the gulf between aboriginals and non-aboriginals in Canada.

Confrontation at Oka, September 1, 1990.

Master Corporal Clayton Matchee poses with tortured Somali prisoner Shidane Arone, March 16, 1993.

89

Shame in Somalia

Searing photos sealed fate of airborne regiment

PETER DESBARATS

This photograph was taken on the night of March 16, 1993. The place was Somalia, a small, troubled and relatively unimportant African nation.

The soldier in the photograph is Master Corporal Clayton Matchee—a member of the Flying Dust First Nation reserve in Saskatchewan—then serving in the Canadian Airborne Regiment. Another Canadian soldier is holding the camera, and Matchee is posing with a bloodied sixteen-year-old Somali called Shidane Arone, who is about to die. The photograph appalled Canadians, destroyed the Canadian Airborne Regiment, and left Matchee unfit to stand trial after a botched suicide attempt. He has never fully recovered.

At the outset of the Somalia mission, Canadians still proudly considered themselves to be a nation of peacekeepers. This tradition dated back to 1956–57 and the leading role played by future Canadian prime minister and Nobel Prize–winner Lester Pearson during the Suez Crisis.

Ever since then, keeping the peace under United Nations auspices had been an important element of Canada's military tradition—although the 1993 mission was different in a number of respects. It was funded by member states, not the U.N. itself, and was commanded by the United States. Its principal role was to provide security for humanitarian organizations trying to cope with the effects of civil war, drought and starvation in Somalia.

Selected for the mission was the 900-member Canadian Airborne Regiment. The choice would prove fatal to the regiment, which had been created in 1968.

There were ominous signs at the outset. Disciplinary problems plagued the regiment in its home base in Petawawa, Ontario. These continued in Somalia.

The Canadians set up camp near the town of Belet Huen and soon faced rampant petty thievery by the locals, culminating in the arrest and detention of Shidane Arone on the night of March 16. Testimony heard at later courts martial claimed that Matchee played a leading role in the extreme physical abuse of Arone that led to his death.

Allegations of a cover-up by officers led to the appointment of a commission of inquiry. The inquiry uncovered evidence of racism in the rank and file as well as episodes of degrading and dehumanizing hazing ceremonies, prompting Defence Minister David Collenette to order the regiment disbanded. By 1997, though, the commission itself became a source of controversy when the Chrétien government prematurely closed it down and forced it to publish an incomplete version of its report.

This photo, and the fifteen others taken during Arone's torture, shattered our faith in the military. It also drove morale to a new low within the Armed Forces.

As Arone sat dying, his last words were allegedly "Canada, Canada." This horrific image made us all take a long, hard look in the mirror.

Clear-Cut Victory

Summary of protest saved old-growth forest

TINA LOO

The mists common to the west coast of Vancouver Island added to the sense of anticipation that ran through the Clayoquot "peace camp" one summer morning in 1993. According to the Mounties assigned to the Kennedy River Bridge, "word from higher up" was that something was about to happen. Something big.

That "something" turned out to be the mass arrest of more than 800 protesters for blockading forestry giant MacMillan Bloedel's logging road. Those arrests and the proceedings that followed—the largest mass trial in the history of the Western world—were key events in British Columbia's battle for the trees. The Clayoquot summer fundamentally changed forest practices, ending the controversial practice of clear-cutting.

Best known for its towering cedars, the Clayoquot rainforest is among the most biologically productive ecosystems in the world and home to a diversity of species. But like temperate rainforests everywhere, those on Vancouver Island were threatened by forestry practices designed with economic productivity in mind: clearcutting, or removing all or most of the trees in an area, allowed logging companies to get as many board feet as possible out of the woods quickly.

The aesthestics of efficiency worked against both the companies and their employees. Photographs of scarred and smouldering landscapes mobilized people to act. The first protests started in the early 1980s, when the provincial government gave MacMillan Bloedel permission to log 90 percent of Meares, one of the larger islands in the sound. Local residents rallied in support of the Clayoquot First Nation, which declared the island a tribal park, bringing a halt to logging.

Meares was only the first skirmish in what would be an ongoing fight to save Clayoquot. After intensive negotiations, in 1993 the government announced that two-thirds of the sound would be opened to logging—a compromise between jobs and the environment. Outraged, environmentalists promised direct action.

Over the summer, some 10,000 people found their way to the protest camp. Their blockade brought logging operations to a standstill and garnered media attention. The mass arrests, along with appearances by celebrities such as Robert F. Kennedy, Jr., and the Australian rock band Midnight Oil, only fuelled interest, transforming Clayoquot into an international symbol of rainforest destruction and Canada into the "Brazil of the North." Capitalizing on the attention, environmental groups rolled out a second strategy in 1994: a marketing campaign aimed at MacMillan Bloedel's customers. Did readers of the *New York Times* know that all the news that was fit to print was circulated on paper made from old-growth forests?

In response to public pressure, and to a report from its own scientists, the provincial government announced an end to clear-cutting in 1995. Shortly afterwards, MacMillan Bloedel transferred its rights in the area to a native-owned logging company, and negotiations were completed that made Clayoquot Sound a UNESCO Biosphere Reserve.

Something big really did happen on the Kennedy River Bridge that summer morning in 1993—evidence of the power of non-violent protest to change the world.

90

Protesters blockade a road during the Clayoquot Sound protests in the summer of 1993.

91

Pro-Canada rally prior to second Quebec referendum, Montreal, October 27, 1995.

Referendum Rally

Did massive pro-Canada rally sway Quebecers?

DESMOND MORTON

By official estimate, 100,000 people gathered in Montreal's Canada Square on Friday, October 27, 1995, opposite the federal government's main office building. As this photo shows, someone provided a huge Canadian flag to encourage patriotic demonstrators. Unofficial "Unity Committee" volunteers handed out placards as the crowd urged Quebecers to vote "No" in the looming referendum and remain part of Canada. Who said Canadians did not care about their country, or that nobody would mind if Quebecers picked up and left?

On October 30, Quebecers lined up to vote in the province's second sovereignty referendum. By nightfall, an incredible 97 percent of eligible voters had cast ballots. Initial reports showed the Yes side for sovereignty well ahead, but the tide slowly turned and, by midnight, the No side was ahead by less than a percentage point. Canada, as we know it, was saved by the kind of narrow margin that normally demands a recount.

Controversy swirled in the wake of the referendum, with questions arising over the thousands of "No" votes that had been declared "spoiled," especially in largely English-speaking ridings. Quebec's chief elections officer, meanwhile, had much bigger questions to ponder: Who had paid for all those No demonstrators who had flooded Montreal the previous Friday? What should he do about non-Quebec politicians and corporations that boasted of their illegal contributions to the pro-Canada rally?

Lost in the arguments was the question of the rally's influence. Had it saved Canada? Federal government polling at the time told a fascinating, but largely secret, story. A week before the vote, polls showed the Yes side in the lead. In the middle of the week, Prime Minister Jean Chrétien promised Quebecers that their constitutional demands would be heard. Quebecers were moved by his words, and, by Thursday, the No side had a 1 percent lead.

Many No-side officials, meanwhile, had deep misgivings about the promised Friday rally. What if it backfired? The truth was, it was too late to cancel it. On the day of the rally, French-language television reported tiny crowds. Then Radio Canada aired an interview with a man who claimed the rally was condescending, even insulting. Many in Quebec heard the interview and agreed. The polls dipped. Suddenly, the No side was losing again!

Quebec Premier Jacques Parizeau, meanwhile, was overjoyed. According to his polls, the Yes side was in the lead. Surely, his dream of a sovereign Quebec would come true on Monday.

The federal government continued polling Quebecers right up to Sunday. By nightfall, their polls were showing the No side back in the lead. Were Quebecers finally responding to the previous Friday's pro-Canada rally?

The No-side victory would have far-ranging impacts. Parizeau promptly resigned as premier in favour of Lucien Bouchard. In Ottawa, Chrétien and Stéphane Dion brought in a Clarity Act—something that most Quebecers favoured—to ensure that any future referenda would have a clear question.

Shawinigan Handshake

Prime minister's gripping moment startled Canadians

DON NEWMAN

"I took him down!" That is how Prime Minister Jean Chrétien described what happened when a protester confronted him on February 15, 1996.

The protester's name was Bill Clennett, and he was one of a group of activists who had gathered to demonstrate during a speech by the prime minister. The occasion was a special ceremony to mark the thirty-first anniversary of the adoption of the Maple Leaf as the flag of Canada. For the previous thirty years, there had been no Flag Day event. But due to the agonizingly close call in the Quebec referendum four months earlier, the federal government had decided to wave the flag, so to speak, on the anniversary date in 1996.

What's more, the federal ceremony would be held in Quebec—not deep in Quebec, mind you, but in a park near the Ottawa River with a view of Parliament Hill. The event was cobbled together quickly, and was not very well organized. To get to the stage and the microphone, Chrétien had to walk across a portion of the park, through a crowd that included the demonstrators.

It was a brilliant day and sunshine reflected brightly off the snow. It was a day for sunglasses, and Chrétien was wearing his. As dignitaries began speaking, the demonstrators tried their best to disrupt the proceedings. Finally, Chrétien took the microphone. The catcalls and insults grew louder.

"Chrétien au chomage!" they shouted. "Make Chrétien unemployed!"

The prime minister finished his perfunctory remarks and left the stage. Unlike at other speaking events, however, Chrétien didn't linger to shake hands or bask in public attention. Possibly he was still feeling jumpy from a troubling incident that had occurred shortly after the Quebec referendum. An intruder had managed to elude security and break into his official residence in Ottawa, making it all the way to his bedroom before being stopped. Whatever the reason, Chrétien started walking briskly across the park, outpacing the RCMP security detail that was accompanying him. The protesters were still chanting. Suddenly one of them stepped directly into Chrétien's path.

The prime minister didn't hesitate—one hand to the throat, the other behind the protester's head, and Bill Clennett was flat on his back on the ground. Chrétien kept going, and because he was moving so quickly, most photographers were not close enough to the catch the action. The best image of the takedown came from a TV video camera. Reproduced as a still, the image is grainy—but both the action and the message are clear.

Chrétien would later joke about the incident, which became known as the "Shawinigan handshake" after the prime minister's hometown in Quebec. But after that day, things did begin to change. From then on, Chrétien was rarely seen as the convivial "little guy from Shawinigan." Canadians came to see just how tough and unyielding he really was.

Despite the startling incident, Chrétien won two more majority governments. Bill Clennett was charged with a minor offence, released, and was soon out protesting again.

Jean Chrétien's "Shawinigan Handshake," February 15, 1996.

92

Liberal
www.liberal.ca

93

Karen Kain, Winnipeg, 1997.

A Graceful Exit

Beloved ballerina bids farewell with haunting image

BEVERLEY TALLON

One couldn't help but be mesmerized when Karen Kain came on stage.

Canada's prima ballerina began dancing at the age of six—an attempt by her mother to improve her posture. By the time she was eight she knew that ballet would be her life. When she was eleven, she left the comforts of the family home to live in the National Ballet School residences. By nineteen she was the principal dancer with the National Ballet of Canada, replacing an injured Victoria Tennant in *Swan Lake*.

Kain would dance with the greats, including the legendary Rudolf Nureyev. Together with Frank Augustyn, she won first prize for the best pas de deux at the Moscow International Ballet Competition in 1973. When a journalist addressed her as a "prima ballerina" the following year the demure dancer quickly replied, "I wouldn't go that far."

Graceful and disciplined, delicate but strong, Kain could be flung through the air by her dancing partner and return like a feather caught in a whirlwind.

Kain's ballet roles read like a large collection of both full-length and shorter works. She played the title role and the Swan Queen in *Giselle* and became Aurora in *The Sleeping Beauty*. She performed in Frederick Ashton's *La Fille mal gardée* and John Cranko's *Romeo and Juliet*.

Choreographers clamoured to create roles for her. From 1974 onward, Kain was a guest artist of Roland Petit of the Ballet National de Marseille in France. With youthful enthusiasm she made the roles distinctively her own. Later, with the confidence of maturity, she brought a depth and originality like no other.

Kain's success did not come without its share of personal sacrifice and pain; she had to practise up to eight hours a day. In a 1976 CBC interview, she said that in the morning, her ankles felt "like they might shatter" when she walked on them.

What kept her going? "Basically? I really love to dance."

More than two decades later, Kain's name would be among the first to be added to Canada's Walk of Fame. (Kain subsequently said of the inlaid "sidewalk star" in Toronto's Theatre District that she hoped the award would inspire other young dancers.)

But like all great artists and athletes, the time came for Kain to retire from her dancing career. She is shown in this 1997 photograph in Winnipeg after her last performance in a National Ballet production of *Swan Lake*. The dark moodiness of the image captures the finality of the moment.

For many of us, retirement will likely be marked by a modest celebration—perhaps accompanied by a moment of personal reflection. Kain's retirement was in the limelight. She hung up her slippers to thunderous applause. A poignant sadness is revealed in this picture, like a rose captured in a Renaissance painting; such a public figure cannot hide.

Chaos in Quebec City

Summit strife marked last gasp for anti-globalizationists

DON NEWMAN

Canadians had not seen anything like it: waves of masked protesters storming against a steel and concrete barricade; ranks of police in riot gear standing behind the barricade, batons in hand, ready to repel any breach.

On April 20, 2001, Quebec City exploded into a melee of Molotov cocktails, tear gas, rubber bullets, and powerful water cannons, as talks to negotiate a hemispheric free trade deal went on behind the security barricades. The violence during the Summit of the Americas lasted two days, shocking Canadians and garnering international media attention. It led to hundreds of arrests and subsequent complaints that police and security agencies had overreacted.

The Summit of the Americas was a meeting of the leaders of thirty-four countries in North, South, and Central America. Only Cuba was excluded.

It would be the riot, however, and not the negotiations that would dominate headlines. Twenty thousand protesters had descended upon Quebec's historic Old City. The summit came at the height of the anti-globalization movement, which began in the late 1980s and gathered strength in the 1990s. Largely driven by left-leaning agendas, the protesters were united by a common goal—curtailing the power of transnational corporations and of affluent Western nations.

Bracing for the worst, police in Quebec cordoned off the summit site with a large barricade system that would become known as "the fence." The barricade was a by-product of lessons learned from the infamous "Battle in Seattle" where, in 1999, an estimated 40,000 protesters stormed through that city's streets during a meeting of the World Trade Organization.

In Quebec City, protesters and police engaged in a violent game of cat and mouse. Throughout Friday and Saturday, demonstrators rushed the barricade, and in one instance, managed to pull down a portion. The police in turn slammed the protesters with water cannons. Riot squads formed lines and, with a barrage of tear gas, water cannons and rubber bullets, chased the demonstrators away. After the smoke cleared, the rioters regrouped—and the process repeated itself.

The stench of tear gas was everywhere: in the summit meeting halls; in the delegates' hotels; and in the media room, where journalists were transfixed more by the rioting shown on television than by the negotiations. Despite the chaos, the talks went ahead as scheduled—but they didn't produce a free trade deal. Little did the protesters know that Quebec City would mark the beginning of the end of an era of violent anti-globalization protest.

Just three months later, during a large and violent demonstration at the G-8 Summit in Genoa, Italy, one activist was shot to death by police, and hundreds of protesters and police were injured. The death seemed to stun both sides of the anti-globalization issue. The following year, at the G-8 Summit in Kananaskis, Alberta, police and journalists would vastly outnumber protesters. The demonstrations that did take place were peaceful—a direct result, some might say, of the violent legacy of Quebec City and similar protests.

94

Summit of the Americas protest, Quebec City, April 20, 2001.

95

Canada's women's hockey team wins Olympic gold, 2002.

She Shoots, She Scores!

Canadians cheered women's golden moment

RICHARD W. POUND

Women's ice hockey was finally added to the program of the Olympic Winter Games at Nagano, Japan, in 1998. The overwhelming favourite to win the gold medal was Canada, a team that had effectively taught the second-favourite United States how to play the game.

Entering the tournament with eight straight wins against the Americans, the Canadians suffered a numbing defeat against the United States in the final. They would have to wait an agonizing four more years for a chance at redemption.

Back home, Canadians felt the sting of the loss almost as much as the players. Many purists preferred women's Olympic hockey to that played by the overpaid male stars from the NHL and other professional leagues. They considered these women "real" Canadian athletes, struggling for recognition under difficult circumstances. Many of the women sacrificed or postponed their education, families, and careers to train with the team, showing the selfless commitment of the amateurs of bygone days. Everyone could empathize with them and admire their will to overcome the earlier defeat.

The team's highly motivated coach, Danièle Sauvageau, a career police officer, kept the players focused and determined to change the outcome at the next Winter Games in Salt Lake City in 2002. The team's veterans, equally determined, provided a nucleus around which the new challengers could develop their own skills. The level of their hockey improved remarkably.

When the Games finally arrived, the balance of power in women's hockey had shifted. Coming into the tournament, the Americans had a much better record against Canada. Then there were the intangibles: American hockey teams play well at home—indeed, their only Olympic gold medals, both won by men's teams, had come in 1960 in Squaw Valley and the "Miracle on Ice" at Lake Placid in 1980. Could the home team strike gold one more time?

The Salt Lake City final, a rematch between Canada and the United States, was a hard-fought affair. Dubious refereeing by a U.S. official in the last few minutes of the third period—when Canada was clinging to a one-goal lead—seemed virtually designed to produce an equalizer. At the time, the quietly understated Don Cherry said it was the worst refereeing he had ever seen.

Despite this, the Canadians hung on to win, a reward for their tenacious and disciplined play.

The joy displayed in the team's traditional victory photo is infectious, and the squad's strength of character is displayed by the inclusion of Hayley Wickenheiser's young son, Noah, who is sitting on her lap.

The victory proved to be the first of a hockey "double" in Salt Lake City, as the Canadian men won their first gold medal in fifty years. Maybe both teams were inspired by their knowledge that the icemaker had placed a Canadian loonie coin under centre ice.

Controversial Celebration

The kiss heard 'round the world

CHRISTOPHER MOORE

On June 10, 2003, Ontario began issuing marriage licences to same-sex couples. Mike Stark, at left in this photograph, and Michael Leshner, his life partner since 1981, were first in line. Duly licensed, "the Michaels" married in a civil ceremony shortly afterwards. Before an array of cameras and microphones, they celebrated with the kiss heard 'round the world.

Would this photograph top your list as the most shocking image from Canadian history? Or would you see it as the culmination of a struggle for equality fought by gays in Canada?

When gay marriage suddenly became the law of the land, it was the Canadian news event of the year for many commentators. Marriage is a religious sacrament around the world, but marriages have civil and secular consequences too, and every state has regulated marriage. In 1866, a British judge defined marriage as "the voluntary union for life of one man and one woman, to the exclusion of all others." Would this remain the legal definition in Canada for the twenty-first century? Did changing mores—and the Canadian Charter of Rights and Freedoms—require that it be changed? Since no government would legislate full marriage equality, some gay couples turned to the courts.

In January 2001, two Toronto couples, Kevin Bourassa and Joe Varnell, and Anne and Elaine Vautour, were married in a double wedding ceremony. They then sued for the marriage licences Ontario refused to give them. Same-sex couples in British Columbia and in Quebec sued for the same rights.

The courts of Quebec gave the first affirmation of same-sex marriage rights, but no licences were issued, pending an appeal. In May 2003, a British Columbia court found same-sex couples had a right to marry, but it delayed implementation to permit legislated amendments. On June 10, 2003, however, the Ontario Court of Appeal not only decided that same-sex couples had a right to marry, but made the right retroactive to January 2001. That meant the Vautours and Bourassa and Varnell were already married, the first legally married gay couples in the Western world in modern history. Within minutes of the decision, "the Michaels" received the first marriage licence issued to a gay couple in Canada. Soon British Columbia courts cancelled their delay in implementation, and Quebec courts quashed the appeal there.

With gay marriage already established in several provinces, the Supreme Court confirmed the Canadian Parliament's authority to legislate about marriage. The law, it said, was a living tree, and what the courts had said about marriage in the nineteenth century could grow and change. In July 2005 the federal Civil Marriage Act came into force. Throughout Canada, gay couples had the same right to marry as heterosexual couples.

Concepts as profound as love, marriage, and what consenting adults do in public or private can change, sometimes with surprising speed. Homosexuality was a crime in Canada in 1969. Since 2005, Canadian gay couples have faced the same privileges and responsibilities in legal marriage as everyone else.

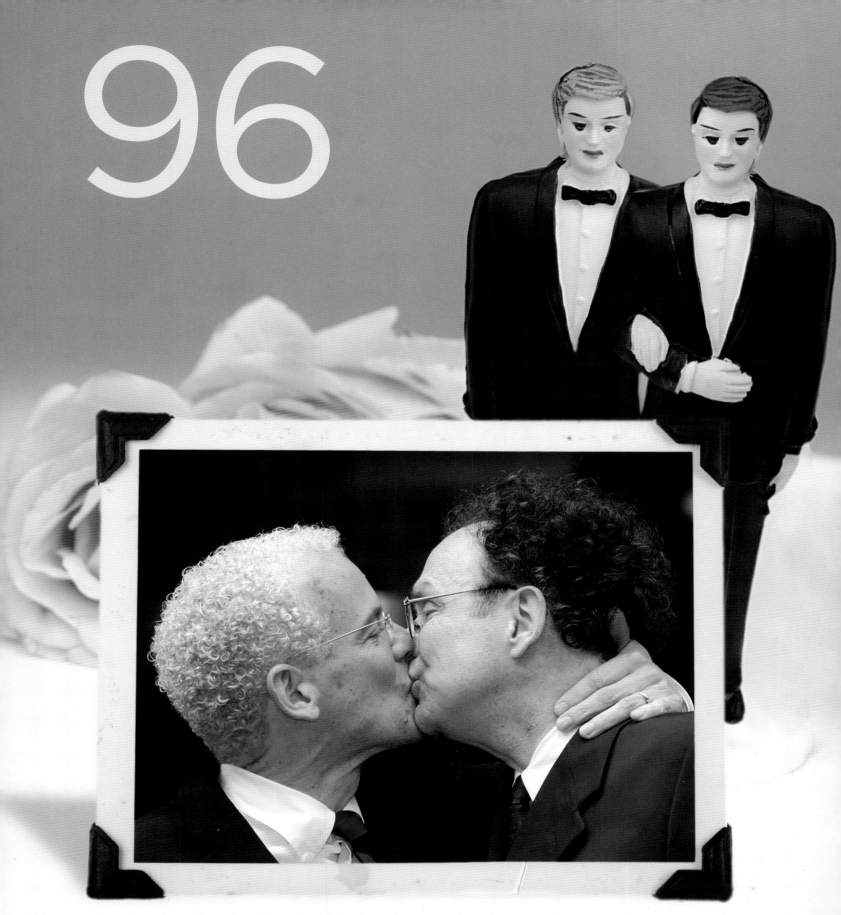

96

Mike Stark (left) and Michael Leshner, the first same-sex couple to receive a marriage licence in Canada, celebrate their wedding in Toronto, June 10, 2003.

97

Funeral for four RCMP officers, Edmonton, March 10, 2005.

Red Serge Sacrifice

The nation mourned murdered Mounties

PETER MANSBRIDGE

Police officers do cry. And on this day in March 2005, they had every reason to. This heart-rending photograph was taken just a week after four RCMP officers had been killed in the town of Mayerthorpe, Alberta.

More than 10,000 people had come to grieve at a memorial service in Edmonton. Overwhelmingly, the seats were occupied by police officers—not just RCMP, but from just about every force in Canada, and many in the United States and beyond. The sadness was palpable.

The storied force had lost officers before in the line of duty, more than 200 to that point in its history. But it had never lost four in a single day, until a man named James Roszko—a violent, bullying, convicted sex offender who loved guns and hated police—ambushed four young constables. So unsuspecting of danger were the officers, so completely taken by surprise, only one of them ever managed to return fire.

At the memorial service, televised live across the country on all the major networks, Prime Minister Paul Martin spoke for all Canadians. "We are left numb," he said, "that a single act of hate has affected so many lives, caused so much grief, interrupted so much love."

Indeed, each of the four officers presented a tragic story: Brock Myrol, 29, had became engaged just five weeks earlier; Leo Johnston, 33, had been married for less than six months; Anthony Gordon, 28, had a young son, and his wife was pregnant again; Peter Schiemann, 25, wasn't supposed to be in Mayerthorpe that day. He was just giving a ride to another officer before heading off for other duties. He wasn't in uniform and wasn't even carrying a gun.

In the years following their murders, there would be questions raised about how the RCMP had handled the case and criticism of how the justice system had handled James Roszko, but this was a day for none of that. It was a day for a nation to consider the sacrifice of four particular men and to pay tribute to a police force intrinsic to the Canadian identity.

To the RCMP officers who were friends of the murdered men, the loss was more than symbolic. Bill Sweeney, the commander of the RCMP in Alberta, stood onstage at the memorial to speak. He may have been looking at the officers shown in this photo, sitting in the front row at the service. "The intensity of our pain," he said, "is beyond description."

A Soldier's Soldier

Canadians shocked by first female combat death

CHRISTIE BLATCHFORD

It was early in Canada's mission to Kandahar that Captain Nichola Goddard was killed in action.

It happened on May 17, 2006. The Canadians had been in southern Afghanistan for only a matter of months; back home, it was just barely beginning to sink in that this really was a war. Goddard was the sixteenth Canadian soldier to die in Afghanistan since 2002, and at the time, only the second to die in battle.

A member of the 1st Regiment, Royal Canadian Horse Artillery, Goddard had been serving as a forward observation officer with the Princess Patricia's Canadian Light Infantry at the time of her death.

Because of her gender—she was the first female Canadian soldier to ever be killed in a combat role—Goddard's death received enormous attention. Her photo, the formal posed shot taken of all departing soldiers lest the worst happen, though that great toothy grin was there, ran on front pages across the country.

Her parents, Sally and Tim, were interviewed, and even in their grief sounded as smart and thoughtful as they are. Later, at Nichola Goddard's funeral in Calgary, her dad recalled the nuanced family discussion—probably not unlike others held throughout Canada—that they had had about the mission in Afghanistan. Tim Goddard remembered arguing that education is the key to development in Afghanistan. His daughter's response was swift: "You can't do that when the bad guys run things, dad. They just shoot you."

The country collectively inhaled: When did girls go to the front lines and get to be gunners? Hell, when did *Canada* send soldiers to the front lines? Who were these articulate people in uniform talking on TV? Who were those comrades who, in Tim Goddard's words, "responded to her death with great vigour and imposed an almost Biblical wrath on those who were responsible for it"—and why was he thanking them?

It was as though with Goddard's death, Canadians began to wake up—not merely to the fact that Kandahar was no peacekeeping or peace making mission, but also to the reality of their army, the men and women in it, and the remarkable families from which they spring.

Nichola Kathleen Sarah Goddard was only twenty-six when she died. She grew up in a military sufficiently egalitarian that a young woman didn't have to develop—as her former commander, Major Anne Reiffenstein, once said ruefully—a chip on her shoulder just to survive.

As an officer, Goddard was gravely serious about her responsibilities to her men. Her parents are quite sure she "would much rather that she die" than lose one of her troops.

This photograph shows her exactly as she was—a young woman comfortable in her own lovely skin; at ease with those she nonetheless commanded and whose welfare was her abiding concern, an ordinary Canadian soldier whose death alerted her country to the honour in soldiering and to the extraordinary nature of those who do it.

98

Captain Nichola Goddard in Afghanistan, April 16, 2006.

99

Governor General Michaëlle Jean taking part in a traditional Inuit ceremony,
April 13, 2008.

One Giant Leap

Blanket toss illustrates changing face of Canada

CHARLOTTE GRAY

If evidence is needed of the dynamic nature of Canada, this photograph provides it. Here are two people, deeply respected within their communities, enjoying a moment of such genuine joy that it leaves viewers smiling as broadly as the enthusiastic crowd at their feet. The man on the right is Abel Tingmiak, a sixty-two-year-old Inuvik elder known as a master of the blanket toss, a traditional Inuit sport. The woman on the left is Governor General Michaëlle Jean. The governor general met Tingmiak on a four-day visit to the Northwest Territories in April 2008. The event was part of a lively afternoon of dancing, drumming, and singing.

Locals declared that no Canadian viceregal had ever starred in an Inuit blanket toss before. That's no surprise. Such a moment of spontaneity—let alone the presence of these two people on the same blanket—would have been inconceivable for most of our history.

Until recently, the roughly 40,000 residents of Canada's scattered Inuit communities rarely saw southerners. Northern distances were too vast, the weather too unpredictable, and the expense too high for most dignitaries to venture across the Arctic Circle. When an outsider did appear, the program was rigidly scripted. Heads of state observed local entertainment from the sidelines.

But that was when our governors general conformed to inflexible standards of ceremonial behaviour. The first seventeen GGs after Confederation in 1867 were all titled British grandees. These men—moustaches bristling and chests sparkling with medals—were relentlessly correct in their public conduct. Since 1952, all our vice-regal representatives have been Canadian citizens. But British traditions of ceremonial spit and polish continued with the first four Canadian GGs.

However, Canada was changing, and so was the elite from whom our vice-regal representatives are drawn. In 1978, we had our first governor general from a background that was neither British nor French: Ed Schreyer, whose parents had arrived from Ukraine. Next came our first female viceregal representative: Jeanne Sauvé. Soon followed the first Acadian, Roméo LeBlanc, and then later, the first Chinese Canadian, Adrienne Clarkson. And in 2005 the role passed to Michaëlle Jean, a broadcaster born in Port-au-Prince, Haiti, who arrived in this country as a refugee when she was eleven years old.

Look at the expressions on the faces of Abel Tingmiak and Her Excellency Michaëlle Jean! Born half a world away from each other, their backgrounds, experiences, and identities could not be more different.

Half a century ago, the story of Canada was told as the story of two peoples, the English and the French. Half a century ago, the Inuit elder's rights as a Canadian citizen were frequently overlooked, while the Haitian refugee claimant might well have been turned away from our shores. Today, the stories of these two laughing people are part of the continuing drama of Canada—a country committed to democracy, accessibility, and fairness for all Canadians.

A Way Forward

Apology the first step on long road to healing

BRIAN MARACLE

By delivering a face-to-face apology to national aboriginal leaders in the House of Commons, Prime Minister Stephen Harper hoped that the long, sad story of residential schools would finally be put to rest. The apology, read in the House on June 11, 2008, came after years of horrific headlines, countless lawsuits, and a snowballing public outcry over the devastating impact of residential schools on Indian people and on Canada's reputation.

Prompted by a Royal Commission, the federal government in 1998 had put nearly $350 million—and then seven years later, another $40 million—into an Aboriginal Healing Foundation. The money was meant to fund local programs geared to redress the effects of years of separation from family and culture, the incidents of physical and sexual abuse, and the resultant calamity and chaos in successive generations. Ottawa later provided individual compensation payments that may total $2 billion.

The apology, money, and programs cannot erase the fact that Indian people were stripped of their language, culture, and ceremonial moorings. Nor can it redress the physical and sexual abuse that occurred at residential schools. Indeed, the wave of binge drinking, drug abuse, and suicides that accompanied the residential school compensation payments shows that much more is needed to achieve true healing. This healing will come about only when aboriginal communities undo the work of the residential schools—schools that were established to "civilize" Indian people and assimilate them into Canadian society. Assimilation, in fact, was government policy for more than a century.

Today, the First Nations peoples of Great Turtle Island are surrounded by more than 30 million non-native Canadians and besieged by elements of non-native culture. They have steadfastly resisted the increasing pressures to assimilate and are fiercely determined to retain their separate and unique identities. To do so for the next hundred years they must remain true to their teachings, and fill the void created by the residential schools by ensuring that their languages, culture, and ceremonies are passed on.

A century from now, the government's apology very well may be forgotten—but the residential schools and their terrible legacy will still be remembered by Indian people. The path to healing and recovery, however, does not dwell on past hurts and injuries—even though those things will never and should never be forgotten. Indian people will be made whole only when they fully recover the things that made them strong in the past: their ties to the land, to each other, and to the Creator.

Fortunately, a cultural renaissance has been underway in Indian country for the past generation. The languages, culture, and ceremonies—the key to survival as a distinct people—are being rejuvenated and reinforced. More and more people are embracing the past and building for the future by living in peace with our Mother the Earth, helping and loving one another, and revering the Creator for all of our blessings.

Residential schools apology, June 11, 2008.

100

ACKNOWLEDGEMENTS

A project of this scope and scale—one hundred photos, one hundred essays, and thirty-seven writers—could not be completed without the help of a legion of talented collaborators.

I would like to offer my deepest thanks to the guest contributors, History Society board members, and *Beaver* editorial team members who wrote the essays that accompany the images: Irving Abella, Thomas Axworthy, Christie Blatchford, Michael Bliss, Jim Burant, Margaret Conrad, Tim Cook, Denys Delâge, Peter Desbarats, Will Ferguson, J.L. Granatstein, Charlotte Gray, Deborah Grey, Rudyard Griffiths, Paul Jones, Phil Koch, Jacques Lacoursière, Tina Loo, Peter Mansbridge, Brian Maracle, Ken McGoogan, Christopher Moore, Deborah Morrison, Desmond Morton, Don Newman, Nelle Oosterom, André Picard, Robert Pichette, Jacques Poitras, Richard W. Pound, Joel Ralph, Graeme Roy, Beverley Tallon, Brian Tobin, Chris Webb, Winona Wheeler, and Brian Young. Your collective efforts, advice, and enthusiasm for the project are much appreciated.

The support and encouragement of Deborah Morrison, president and CEO of Canada's National History Society and publisher of *The Beaver*, was crucial to the success of this project. So, too, was the assistance provided by the entire History Society team—Danielle Chartier, Pat Gerow, James Gillespie, Pat Hanney, Tanja Hutter, Linda Onofreychuk, Joel Ralph, Brian Stendel, and Scott Bullock. A sincere thank you goes out to dedicated *Beaver* editorial staff members Phil Koch, Nelle Oosterom, and Beverley Tallon, who helped copy-edit the book, as well as to art director Michel Groleau, who designed our "10 Photos That Changed Canada" magazine feature and came up with the original montage concepts that accompanied the photos. Five of his original montages—The Last Spike; Wait for Me, Daddy; Henderson's Goal; Terry Fox; and Standoff at Oka—appear in this book. Thanks also to the photography experts who helped us select the original "10 Photos That Changed Canada"— Michael Creagen, George Diack, Moe Doiron, Ric Ernst, and Barry Gray. My gratitude, as well, to the photographers whose images started it all: William Ivor Castle, Peter Martin, Doug Ball, Rod MacIvor, Shaney Komulainen, Alexander J. Ross, Claude Detloff, Frank Lennon, Robert Nadon, and Fred Davis.

The support I have received from the History Society's board of directors—James Baillie, J. Douglas Barrington, Margaret Conrad, Charlotte Gray, Robert Johnston, Paul Jones, Jacques Lacoursière, Gillian Manning, Don Newman, Richard W. Pound, H. Sanford Riley, David Ross, and Brian Young—is much appreciated.

During the creation of *100 Photos That Changed Canada*, I had the pleasure of collaborating with several members of HarperCollins Canada's team, including Phyllis Bruce, photo editor Barbara Kamienski, managing editor Noelle Zitzer, art director Alan Jones, and marketing manager Charidy Johnston. I'm very grateful for their professionalism and enthusiasm.

Choosing one hundred iconic Canadian photos is no easy task. During the selection process, I relied on the advice and expertise of a host of historians, archivists, and photography experts. To everyone who helped me during the selection process, thank you. Thank you as well to Library and Archives Canada, The Canadian Press, and the host of archives and individual image providers who helped us complete this special project. A full list can be found on the photo credits page.

On a more personal note, it would not have been possible to tackle a project like this one without the support and encouragement of my family. I want especially to thank my parents, Peter and Diane Reid; my wife's parents, Michael and Susan Helm; as well as my wife, Marianne Helm, and our children, Evan and Megan. It was Marianne, a professional photographer, who first suggested that *The Beaver* publish an article on iconic Canadian photos. Without her, none of this would have been possible.

—Mark Reid

CONTRIBUTORS

Irving Abella is the Shiff Professor of Canadian Jewish History at York University and the Distinguished Senior Fellow of Canadian Studies at the University of Ottawa. The author or co-author of eight books, including *None Is Too Many* and *A Coat of Many Colours: Two Centuries of Jewish Life in Canada*, he is also a past-president of the Canadian Jewish Congress and the Canadian Historical Association.

Thomas S. Axworthy is the former Senior Policy Advisor and Principal Secretary to Prime Minister Trudeau. He became a Fellow, and then Mackenzie King Chair of Canadian Studies, Harvard (1984–99); Executive Director, Historica Foundation, initiator of the Heritage Minutes (1999–2005); and is current Chair, Centre for the Study of Democracy, Queen's University. He is an Officer of the Order of Canada (2002) and was also awarded the Public Affairs Association Award of Distinction (2008).

Christie Blatchford is a national columnist with the *Globe and Mail*. Her 2007 book on the war in Afghanistan, *Fifteen Days: Stories of Bravery, Friendship, Life and Death from Inside the New Canadian Army*, won the 2008 Governor General's Literary Award for Non-fiction.

Michael Bliss is University Professor Emeritus at the University of Toronto and the author of numerous books on Canadian history and the history of medicine.

Jim Burant graduated with a Master's in Art History from Carleton University, and has been working for Library and Archives Canada in various capacities since 1976. He has published widely, organized numerous exhibitions, and has an international reputation in the archival and art communities. A recipient of the Queen's Jubilee Medal in 2003, he is an off-reserve member of the Algonquins of Pikwakanagan First Nation, and is married with two children.

Margaret Conrad, OC, FRSC, holds the Canada Research Chair in Atlantic Canada Studies at the University of New Brunswick. A former Chair of Canada's National History Society, she has published widely in the fields of Canadian history and women's studies. She is the coordinator of the Atlantic Canada Portal, designed to support and showcase research on the history and culture of Atlantic Canada.

Tim Cook is the First World War historian at the Canadian War Museum and an Adjunct Research Professor at Carleton. He has published four books, including the two-volume history of Canadians fighting in the Great War, *At the Sharp End* and *Shock Troops*, which have been awarded the 2007 J.W. Dafoe prize and the 2008 Charles Taylor Prize for Literary Non-fiction.

Denys Delâge is Emeritus Professor in the department of sociology at Laval University. He works mainly on the French and British networks of alliances that were centred in Montreal and expanded towards the Great Lakes and the Mississippi. He published *Bitter Feast: Amerindians and Europeans in Northeastern North America, 1600–64* (UBC Press). A member of the Société des Dix, he has published articles on the history of dogs in the colonial encounter, on colonial models and the dynamics of alliance and conquest, and on history and the colonial legacy.

Peter Desbarats spent thirty years as a print and television journalist before being appointed Dean of Journalism at the University of Western Ontario in 1981. He retired in 1997, but continues to teach, write and research. In 2007 he was appointed an Officer of the Order of Canada.

Will Ferguson was born in Fort Vermilion, Alberta, a former fur trading post closer to the Arctic Circle than the American border. He has won the Stephen Leacock Medal for Humour twice and was awarded the Pierre Berton Award by Canada's National History Society in 2005. Ferguson is the author of several bestselling books on Canadian travel, culture, and history, including *Canadian History for Dummies* and *Beauty Tips from Moose Jaw: Travels in Search of Canada*. He lives in Calgary with his wife, Terumi, and their two sons, Alex and Alister.

J.L. Granatstein taught history for thirty years, is a Senior Research Fellow of the Canadian Defence and Foreign Affairs Institute, was Director and CEO of the Canadian War Museum, and writes on Canadian history, foreign policy and defence, and politics. Among his publications are *The Ottawa Men* and *A Man of Influence*.

Charlotte Gray is the author of seven non-fiction bestsellers, including biographies of Alexander Graham Bell and Nellie McClung, and the winner of numerous awards, including the Pierre Berton Award for popularizing Canadian history. The Chair of Canada's National History Society, Gray is also member of the Order of Canada, and frequently appears on Canadian television and radio.

Deborah Grey, OC MP (Ret'd), served as the first Reform MP in the House of Commons from 1989 to 2004. As a high school English teacher in northeast Alberta, she saw many sights similar to the photo of John Diefenbaker in his "Final Farewell." She and her husband, Lewis Larson, divide their time between Edmonton and Vancouver Island.

Rudyard Griffiths is co-founder of the Dominion Institute, a national non-profit organization dedicated to the promotion of Canadian history and civic literacy. A columnist with the *National Post*, Griffiths has edited seven collections of essays on Canadian political and historical themes and is the author of *Who We Are: A Citizen's Manifesto* (2009). In 2006, the *Globe and Mail* recognized Griffiths as one of Canada's "Top 40 Under 40."

Paul Jones is an award-winning writer, speaker and business consultant with clients across North America. During thirty years with Maclean Hunter and Rogers, he published leading magazines and served as director of many organizations. He holds the highest honours conferred by both magazine and advertising industry associations, and is also a director of Canada's National History Society, an accredited genealogist, and a committed genealogical volunteer.

Phil Koch writes, edits, and studies in Winnipeg, where he is the assistant editor of *The Beaver* and a University of Manitoba graduate student in religion, English, and architecture. He co-founded and co-edited the culture magazine *Tart* and is the winner of the 2006 Canadian Association of University Teachers Award for Excellence in Education Journalism.

Jacques Lacoursière is a popular historian, broadcaster and author of many books about Canadian history. A director of Canada's National History Society, he has been involved in history education and curriculum development in the province of Quebec. He is a recipient of the Pierre Berton Award, a member of the Order of Canada, and a Knight of the National Order of Quebec.

Tina Loo teaches environmental history at the University of British Columbia, where she holds a Canada Research Chair. She has written about wildlife conservation in Canada and is currently looking at the social and environmental impacts of hydroelectric development in B.C. As one of the presenters with Al Gore's Climate Project, she facilitates public discussions about global warming and solutions to it—in return for bus fare.

Peter Mansbridge is the Chief Correspondent of CBC News. In forty years with the CBC, Mansbridge has provided coverage of the most significant stories in Canada and around the world. He has received twelve Gemini Awards, and has also received six honorary degrees from universities across the country. He has also been recognized by leading universities in the United States and the United Kingdom. In 2008, Mansbridge was made an Officer of the Order of Canada. Born in London, England, in 1948, Mansbridge was educated in Ottawa and served in the Royal Canadian Navy in 1966 and 1967.

Brian Maracle is the author of *Crazywater: Native Voices on Addiction and Recovery* (1994) and *Back on the Rez: Finding the Way Home* (1996). He lives with his wife, Audrey, on the Six Nations Grand River Territory where he teaches Kanyen'kéha (the "Mohawk" language) and is active in the Mohawk Longhouse.

Ken McGoogan is the best-selling author of *Fatal Passage, Ancient Mariner, Lady Franklin's Revenge,* and *Race to the Polar Sea.* His awards include the Writers' Trust of Canada Drainie-Taylor Biography Prize, the University of British Columbia Medal for Biography, and the Pierre Berton Award for History from Canada's National History Society. *Fatal Passage* was turned into a docudrama for the BBC and History Channel.

Christopher Moore (www.christophermoore.ca) is a Toronto-based writer, historian, and blogger, and a longtime columnist on history and historians for *The Beaver*.

Deborah Morrison is the President and CEO of Canada's National History Society. She is also the publisher of *The Beaver* and *Kayak: Canada's History Magazine for Kids*, which she launched in 2004. Prior to joining the History Society in 2002, she had a long and distinguished career developing history-related programs as Director of Operations for Historica Foundation of Canada and as Director of Communications for The CRB Foundation.

Desmond Morton has published forty books on Canada's military, political and labour history. He has taught at the University of Toronto Mississauga and at McGill University, and retired in 2005.

Don Newman was the Senior Parliamentary Editor for CBC Television News. He retired in June 2009. He has worked in both broadcasting and print journalism and served as both a national and foreign correspondent. He was the editor and host of the CBC Newsworld program *Politics*. Don Newman lives in Ottawa, and is a member of the Order of Canada and a life member of the Canadian Parliamentary Press Gallery.

Nelle Oosterom is the Associate Editor of *The Beaver: Canada's History Magazine*. She has had a distinguished career as a writer, editor, and broadcaster at The Canadian Press, CBC, Canwest News Service and various newspapers. She has lived and worked in Winnipeg, St. John's, Thunder Bay, and southern Ontario's Niagara Peninsula, and has travelled extensively abroad.

André Picard is the public health reporter at the *Globe and Mail* and the author of three best-selling books.

Dr. Robert Pichette is an Acadian writer and columnist who wrote for the *Globe and Mail* and New Brunswick's principal daily, the *Telegraph-Journal*. After service in the RCAF, he became Deputy Minister to the late Louis J. Robichaud when he was Premier of New Brunswick (1960–1970). Deeply interested in Acadian history, he has written more than twenty books on the subject, one of which was awarded the Prix France-Acadie.

Jacques Poitras is the provincial affairs reporter for CBC News in New Brunswick. He also teaches journalism part-time at St. Thomas University. He is the author of *Beaverbrook: A Shattered Legacy* and *The Right Fight: Bernard Lord and the Conservative Dilemma*, and winner of two Atlantic Book Awards. His work has been recognized by the National Newspaper Awards, the Radio and Television News Directors Association, and Amnesty International.

Richard W. Pound is a director of Canada's National History Society, Chancellor of McGill University and a published author of several historical and biographical works. A partner with the national law firm Stikeman Elliott, he has had a long association with the Olympic Movement as an Olympic swimmer, president of the Canadian Olympic Committee, member of the International Olympic Committee and Chairman of the World Anti-Doping Agency.

Joel Ralph is the Manager of Education and Outreach Programs for Canada's National History Society and a graduate of the Master's in Public History Program at the University of Western Ontario. As a student at the International Study Centre in England, he explored Canadian battlefields, including the beach at Dieppe. He writes for *The Beaver* and blogs about history education and technology. Joel lives in Winnipeg with his wife, Jessie.

Mark Reid is Editor of *The Beaver: Canada's History Magazine*. An award-winning journalist, he has worked as an editor, reporter, and photographer for Canwest News Service, the *Calgary Herald*, the New Brunswick *Telegraph-Journal*, and the Saint John *Times Globe*. Mark also launched and edited *OnCampus*, the University of Calgary's the award-winning newspaper and quarterly magazine. A graduate of Dalhousie University and the University of King's College, Mark lives in Winnipeg with his wife, Marianne Helm, and their children, Evan and Megan.

Graeme Roy is the Director of News Photography for The Canadian Press. He has overseen coverage for everything from political summits, elections, Papal visits, Olympics, and other major sporting events over a twenty-five-year career.

Beverley Tallon lives in Winnipeg and works on the editorial team of *The Beaver: Canada's History Magazine*. She is a former editor of *@ltitude (Western Canada Aviation Museum)* and an award-winning artist with a penchant for history, gardening, and travel.

Hon. Brian V. Tobin, P.C., served as the Federal Minister of Industry from October 2000 to January 2002. Previously he served as the Premier of Newfoundland and Labrador from 1996 to 2000. He served as a Member of Parliament from 1980 to 1996 and served as Minister of Fisheries and Oceans in the federal cabinet from 1993 to 1996. He is currently Senior Business Advisor with Fraser Milner Casgrain LLP in Toronto.

Chris Webb is a journalist, activist and photographer living in Winnipeg. His work has appeared in *New Internationalist, Canadian Dimension, The Beaver* and the *Winnipeg Free Press*. He is currently Publishing Assistant at *Canadian Dimension* magazine.

Winona Wheeler teaches at Athabasca University's Centre for World Indigenous Knowledge and Research. She is a member of the Fisher River Cree First Nation (Manitoba), though her family hails from George Gordon's First Nation in Saskatchewan. A life-long student of indigenous histories, anti-colonial theory, treaty rights, and traditional indigenous knowledge, Winona has been teaching and publishing in indigenous studies since 1988.

Brian Young teaches Quebec history at McGill University and is perhaps best known for his biography of Father of Confederation George-Étienne Cartier, and for his co-authored *Short History of Quebec*. A native of Winnipeg and a board member of Canada's National History Society since 2006, his interests range from vegetable gardening and French food to the history of elites and of Quebec museums.

PHOTO CREDITS

73	The "Bye-Bye Boogie," 1979	The Canadian Press
74	A Final Farewell, 1979	Bob Olsen, Toronto Star/The Canadian Press
75	Until Next Time! 1980	The Canadian Press
76	Terry's Journey, 1980	Peter Martin/The Canadian Press
77	Canuck Comedy Takes Off, ca. 1980–81	Everett Collection/The Canadian Press
78	Signing Off, 1982	Ron Bull/The Canadian Press
79	Star-Struck Scientist, 1984	The Canadian Press
80	Call to Action, 1985	© Dimo Safari
81	The Shamrock Summit, 1985	Scott Applewhite/The Canadian Press
82	White Wolf, 1987	© Jim Brandenburg
83	The Trade, 1988	Ray Giguere/The Canadian Press
84	Tarnished Gold, 1988	Stan Behal/Sun Media Corporation
85	Horror and Heartbreak, 1989	© Allen McInnis, The Gazette (Montreal)
86	Act of Defiance, 1990	Wayne Glowacki/The Canadian Press
87	Naked Ambition, 1990	Barbara Woodley/Labatt Breweries of Canada/Library and Archives Canada, PA-186869. Acquired with the assistance of a grant from the Minister of Communications under the terms of the Cultural Property Import and Export Review Act © Barbara Woodley 1990
88	Standoff at Oka, 1990	Shaney Komulainen/The Canadian Press
89	Shame in Somalia, 1993	Pte. Kyle Brown/Getty Images
90	Clear-Cut Victory, 1993	Mark van Manen/The Vancouver Sun
91	Referendum Rally, 1995	Ryan Remiorz/The Canadian Press
92	The Shawinigan Handshake, 1996	Phil Nolan, Global News/Courtesy of Global Ontario, a division of Canwest Television Limited Partnership
93	A Graceful Exit, 1997	Fred Greenslade/The Canadian Press
94	Chaos in Quebec City, 2001	Paul Chiasson/The Canadian Press
95	She Shoots, She Scores! 2002	Kevork Djansezian/The Canadian Press
96	Controversial Celebration, 2003	Frank Gunn/The Canadian Press
97	Red Serge Sacrifice, 2005	Larry MacDougal/The Canadian Press
98	A Soldier's Soldier, 2006	Murray Brewster/The Canadian Press
99	One Giant Leap, 2008	Fred Chartrand/The Canadian Press
100	A Way Forward, 2008	Fred Chartrand/The Canadian Press

Montage background photos reproduced courtesy of:

14	notes	photo archives, Alexander Graham Bell National Historical Site, Baddeck, N.S.
17	map	courtesy of Barbara Kamienski
27	Ethel Catherwood stamp	© Canada Post Corporation {1996}. Reproduced with permission
34	royal family memento	courtesy of Phyllis Bruce
47	cartoon	Jueland, The Independent, May 21, 1948
69	Trudeau with Castro	Fred Chartrand / The Canadian Press
	Trudeau funeral	Paul Chiasson / The Canadian Press
76	Terry Fox stamp	© Canada Post Corporation {1996}. Reproduced with permission
98	Memorial Cross	Reproduced with the permission of Veterans Affairs Canada, 2009

INDEX